LONDON TRANSPORT

BUSES & COACHES

1959

LONDON TRANSPORT
BUSES & COACHES

1959

John A.S. Hambley

Published in 2000 by
JOHN A.S. HAMBLEY
7 Linden Road,
Dunstable,
Beds. LU5 4NZ

Additional text and research by David A. Ruddom

British Library Cataloguing in Publication Data
A catalogue record for this book is available from the British Library

ISBN 0 9533146 4 2

Designed and produced by Hedgehog.
Printed and bound in Great Britain.

Carshalton garaged RT543 is seen at Mitcham on Christmas Day in use as a trolleybus replacement. Careful inspection of the route blind reveals the route number has been deleted. As a trolleybus depot Carshalton had always provided a special service at the southern end of Route 630 on Christmas Day but during the year under review conversion to motor bus operation had taken place. The 630 remained trolleybus operated at Christmas and therefore Carshalton provided RT buses for the usual special service. Unfortunately for some unknown reason it was decided not to display the 630 number which was removed before the buses went into service. (A.B.Cross)

Acknowledgments

A cordial thanks to all who have continued to support me with this series of books. It is very gratifying to realise that so many enthusiasts and historians of London Transport appreciate the publication of each volume. Correspondence and the continued undiscovered photographers that come forward confirm the interest which the publication of previously unseen material generates. To all I extend a special word of thanks for allowing me the use of your valued material. In this volume these include: James H.Aston, Dave Berwick, Bespix, Colin Bull, C.Carter, Alan B.Cross, Michael Dryhurst, John Gascoine, J.C.Gillham, Ray A.Golds, Roger Holmes, Fred W.Ivey, the late D.W.K.Jones, Kevin Lane, the late Bill Legg, P.D.Long, Laurence Mallett, Pat J.Malsher, Alan Mortimer, A.D.Packer, Tony R.Packer, Douglas F.Parker, R.B.Partridge, the late John H.Price, Michael Rooum, David A.Ruddom, R.H.G.Simpson, John G.S.Smith, Ray Stanmore, Michael A.Sutcliffe and Ron Wellings.

Various publications produced by The London Historical Research Group of the Omnibus Society, The London Omnibus Traction Society, The PSV Circle and The RT/RF Register have been used in the compilation of this volume. Expansion of the information contained within these pages has been provided by a number of experts in their particular fields and I sincerely hope I have thanked all those who have unselfishly given their time to answer my sometimes very awkward queries. As with earlier volumes I must single out my very good friend David Ruddom for special mention. Without his untiring patience and understanding, not to mention time, the books would be all the poorer, especially in the compilation of the captions. My wife Iris and David's wife Enid continue to show great tolerance towards the many hours which have been spent away from them while we cogitate over the accuracy of each book. A big thank you to a pair of very understanding ladies!

Publisher's Note

With such a wealth of photographic material available for 1959, it has been decided not to include a supplement covering earlier years. However please do not feel inhibited from sending material for years already published since additions to the selection of interesting prints waiting to be used are always welcome and will be included as soon as opportunity arises. In this volume once again some photographs have been used which lack any identification as to their original source. For the moment they are credited to the collection from which they were obtained. If thereby credit to any photographer has been inadvertently omitted, I can only apologise profusely and would ask that they contact me so that the omission can be rectified in a future volume. Prints from negatives loaned to me have all been produced by Kevin Lane, who can be thoroughly recommended for all your black and white printing requirements at very competitive rates. He can be contacted at 15 Beech Green, Dunstable, Beds., LU6 1EB. It only leaves me to say that I hope you enjoy this volume and that you will find some long lost memories rekindled.

Introduction

The year was marked by the start of the trolleybus replacement programme which commenced in March. Due to the late delivery of production Routemasters and the surplus of vehicles available, RTs and RTLs were used for the replacement motor bus routes on the first three stages. At the year-end 184 RMs had been delivered to the Executive from the Park Royal factory which enabled the final replacement changeover for the year to use the vehicles of the class for the purpose for which they were initially intended. From June through to October a small number of the class entered passenger service on a number of routes not associated with the trolleybus replacement programme. This was to gain experience with the operating characteristics of the new bus. Ironically nineteen vehicles of the RT class entered public service for the first time during the year, having been in long term storage since delivery in 1954.

Mileage cuts throughout the network continued to be prevalent during the year resulting in an overall fall in the number of passenger vehicles owned compared to the final figures of the previous year. During the first few months of the year a total of forty RT and four RLH buses were outshopped from overhaul in red livery, having entered work in Country Area green. More unexpected was the overhaul and change of colour scheme from red to green of eighteen RTL buses in the second half of the year. They were to remain unique and by the end of the year had still not entered passenger service. Conversion of Country Area RF buses to OMO configuration was completed during the year with a start being made on Central Area examples though their entry into service was deferred due to Trade Union opposition. The five GS class buses which had been on loan to Great Yarmouth Corporation to pioneer OMO services in that town since September of the previous year were returned in July and were immediately put into store at Gillingham Street, Victoria garage.

A total of 212 buses were disposed of during the year amounting to 121 RTLs, 12 RTs, 50 TDs and 29 Ts. For completeness, although outside the scope of this series of books, 408 trolleybuses were withdrawn almost exclusively for scrap amounting to something in the region of 25% of the fleet. 168 of the disposed total of buses were exported to Ceylon, while Jersey Motor Transport and Walsall Corporation took eight and five respectively of the RTL class. Trolleybus 260 was donated to the Museum of British Transport at Clapham in September but in May 1961 was substituted by 1253. It then passed to the London Trolleybus Preservation Society who have maintained it ever since and it is now based at the East Anglia Transport Museum at Carlton Colville near Lowestoft.

As far as route developments go the main emphasis was on the replacement of trolleybuses. This was achieved by a large degree of integration with motor bus routes. True there were straight replacements such as the 96 for the 696 between Woolwich and Dartford but in many cases existing routes were used by enhancement and extension or diversion. A good example of this was the replacement in April of trolleybuses 555 and 581 by strengthening the 38, re-routing the 38A and extending 170.

The Country Area year was marked by the opening of new garages at Hatfield and Stevenage which enabled the closure of the old garages at these places together with Hitchin. In addition Watford High Street closed and all the Watford routes were concentrated on Garston. All this resulted in route reallocations and alterations in these areas. Other than that the summer and winter programmes produced the usual selection of chops and changes including two routes in Grays which bucked the trend and were converted back to crew operation.

1957 had been relatively uneventful and 1958 had been traumatic with the long strike in May and the consequential service cuts in the autumn. 1959 proved to be even more eventful but in a much more positive fashion, although the many enthusiasts of trolleybus travel may not think so.

Awaiting its entry into service just over a fortnight later, RM82 is parked inside Poplar depot on 26th October. Alongside are active and stored trolleybuses, at least one on the right appears to be one of the South African vehicles made redundant at Ilford on 19th August. The first true production examples of the RM class had been delivered in May of the year under review and by the year's end no fewer than 184 were in London Transport hands, though not all were in service. (Bespix)

Reeves Corner at Croydon is now a stop on the Tramlink but on 28th March 1959 part of the electric infra-structure has been tied off above the RT on Route 157 because the route has now replaced the 654 trolleybus to Crystal Palace along with the 154. The wires are still alive round the corner into Lower Church Street for the 630 route for the time being at least for another fifteen months. RT2952, which is heading into Tamworth Road, has been a Merton vehicle since new in November 1952 but in January 1960 the fleet number ended its association with AL, reappearing after overhaul at Enfield. (J.H.Price)

Soon after Route 364 had been transferred from Hitchin operation to Luton RF576 is seen in Park Square, Luton prior to departure on a short journey to Flamstead Village. The closure of the old Stevenage and Hitchin garages with the opening of the purpose built garage at Stevenage on 15th April had resulted in a number of changes to local routes. Route 364 which had previously operated between Hitchin and Luton was extended to cover the withdrawal of the Luton to Flamstead service 356. Two RF buses were transferred from Hitchin to Luton accordingly although this particular example was not one of them. (A.Mortimer)

RT1046 is soon to depart on 10th January from Orpington Station on a journey to Chelsfield on Route 854. The via point blind lists practically all the roads to be traversed en-route to its destination which is only a little over two miles away. (A.R.Packer)

RM110 is seen in Commercial Road in use on new route 5A, which operated on a Monday to Friday only basis between West India Docks and Clerkenwell Green. The service had been introduced with the fourth stage of the conversion from trolleybuses to motor buses on 11th November, replacing peak hour journeys on trolleybus 567 between Smithfield or Aldgate and West India Docks together with Clerkenwell Green short workings on 665. (D.Berwick)

The turmoil of the previous year included the introduction in November of a new Sunday service numbered 134A which followed the parent number from Victoria to Whetstone. It then provided the local service through East Barnet, New Barnet, High Barnet and Mays Lane to Chesterfield Road formerly served by the 34 which became weekdays only. Holloway garaged RT2804 heads for the outer terminal on 22nd March in Junction Road, Highgate passing a very traditional Woolworth's shop front. In December the bus would enter Aldenham for overhaul and the fleet number returned to service at Uxbridge, ending its three years at this north London garage which then only housed the RT type bus. (A.R.Packer)

The deserted forecourt of London Bridge station on Sunday 27th December plays host to Saunders bodied RT3922 turning short before returning to South Croydon garage. At this time the Sunday service on Route 133 worked through to Hendon Central but the southern end enjoyed a more frequent headway. (W.R.Legg)

Parked in the vicinity of Poplar garage, RM66 is fitted for service on the Sunday working of Route 9 for which Poplar provided ten RMs. Due to many teething troubles several of the original allocation to PR were quickly withdrawn, being replaced by newly delivered vehicles. This RM was one of those withdrawn, not re-entering service until early 1960 from West Ham. (J.A.S.Hambley collection)

Alperton garage was the home for RT4011 upon its re-entry into service after the second overhaul it received in December 1958 through to its next visit to works in November 1962. Here on 15th July it stands at Claremont Road, West Kilburn having turned short on Route 187, which ran from South Harrow to Hampstead Heath. The front corner panel advertising announces the visit of the Moscow State Circus to Wembley. (R.A.Golds)

On 16th July RM32 negotiates Trafalgar Square on its Route 11 journey to Liverpool Street. The production RMs that are shown in this book all depict the vehicles prior to the various changes associated with improving the frontal appearance. (R.B.Partridge)

A mobile staff canteen and Queen Elizabeth's Hunting Lodge complete the picture at Chingford which has RT2885 as its centrepiece. Having first entered service in May 1952 garaged at Enfield, this RT would move to New Cross after its second overhaul during August of the year under review. In this May view route blinds have been re-set for a journey on Route 205 to Hammond Street, once renowned for the many glass houses that abounded there but which are now very rapidly being replaced by new housing. (R.A.Golds)

June 10th of the year under review witnessed the withdrawal of the New Barnet Station to Hertford route, 342 and its replacement by an extension of the 350 and 350A. RF610 is seen leaving New Barnet Station destined for Hertford Bus Station with one passenger. The sparse passenger traffic encountered on this route had been confirmed in the middle of October 1957 when it was converted to one-person RF operation. (R.Wellings)

New route 154 utilised a maximum of fifteen buses all working from the newly converted Carshalton garage. A further complement of RTs was also maintained at the new garage for use on route 157 which was shared with Merton. With declining services and rationalisation the Carshalton premises only operated buses from the first stage of the trolleybus conversion programme on 4th March of the year under review until closure on 28th January 1964. RT1380, seen at Crystal Palace during April, was one of the initial allocation, which included many roof box examples, all of which had previously been in store throughout the system in readiness for their new duties. (A.Mortimer)

During its lengthy career with both London Transport and the newly formed London Country Bus Services after 1st January 1970, GS33 spent two sojourns at Tring garage. On its first visit it is seen at Aldbury village with route blind still to be re-set for its return to town on Route 387. In January 1954 this had been the last route to be operated by the C class Leyland Cubs. The Guy Special replacements, as illustrated here, in turn lost the operation in June 1962.

(R.Wellings)

The main service on Route 150 was between Ilford Station and Chigwell Row although a few weekday journeys ventured to the northern extremities of Hainault Forest at Lambourne End as did a more regular Sunday service. Parked on the stand in York Road, Ilford deserted RT244 waits to journey to Chigwell Row, Maypole Inn while passengers disembark from an arrival behind and head for Cranbrook Road. (A.R.Packer)

Shown in this one picture are the two 700 series Green Line routes long associated with Aylesbury from June 1946 when this type of operation recommenced after World War II through to last operation in February 1969 for the 707 and April 1977 for the 706. Both coaches garaged at Chelsham wait departure from Aylesbury town centre for Westerham and Oxted respectively with RF183 parked in front of RF249. (A.Mortimer)

The two closely sited bus stands in York Road, Ilford allow for the segregation of the several routes departing this point. In this scene, almost unbelievable in its lack of parked cars, RT520 waits departure to Turnpike Lane Station sometime in April. Leyton garage assumed responsibility for this RT soon after its last overhaul carried out in March of the year under review. Its last year of operation however was spent at Twickenham before withdrawal in June 1963 and eventual sale to the Societé Commerciale de la Malouine, St.Malo, France. (A.R.Packer)

RT4189 had been transferred to Garston on the closure of Watford High Street garage in April of the year under review only to enter Aldenham for overhaul in October thereby concluding its short stay at the newer premises. At the Watford Junction station bus stop, with the Clarendon Hotel behind, it pauses on its journey from Leavesden to New Barnet Station. The two nearest cars in the car park are both Rileys, the nearer being a pre-war example first registered in March 1939 while the other is a post-war built 'Pathfinder' model. Trees and grass occupy the site of the present day station buildings. (J.A.S.Hambley collection)

It appears the crew have somewhat hurriedly abandoned RT1190 at the end of the long journey from Chipstead Valley on the Sunday only Route 59. The date is 22nd March and the West End Green, West Hampstead terminal has shown little change over the years. (A.R.Packer)

GS48 was scrapped in January 1965 but six years earlier it is seen at Dartford on 14th February working the 452 which ran on Saturdays and Sundays only between this point and West Kingsdown. Rather oddly the route was worked by Northfleet garage rather than Dartford and the bus worked back to its garage at night on Route 450. RT4049 stands abandoned further along the road with minimal route information displayed for Route 477, its crew probably having disappeared into Dartford garage, outside which the picture is taken. (A.R.Packer)

The ever convenient photographic location of the Golders Green Station forecourt finds RT380, now carrying bodywork built by Saunders, waiting departure on Route 83 to Alperton. Passengers were allowed to board buses on stand but no facilities were provided for them to wait if no bus was present and a rather hazardous trip had to be made across the cobbles to reach the vehicle. (J.Gascoine collection)

RT984 waits in St. Albans Street, Windsor in this March scene before it departs for Uxbridge by way of Route 457A. This route followed its unsuffixed counterpart, deviating only on the eastern outskirts of Slough to traverse the Upton Lea area. After overhaul in April of the following year and re-entry into service at Northfleet garage, the RT would eventually be disposed of in February 1964. (A.R.Packer)

The Norwich Union Assurance Society's building at Uxbridge Station bus terminus provides the backdrop to RT911 while employed on Route 204 which ran to Hayes Station. Thirty years later this was to become the U4 service. With an overhaul in November of the year under review this RT3 body found further use with a different fleet number. Of interest is the advertising which, even down to the slipboard, exhorts one to 'Hop on a Bus'. (A.R.Packer)

The distinguishing shape of the roof of Slough Station is seen in the background of RT1023 which is attracting passengers for a journey on local route 446 sometime in April. The lofty telegraph pole visible above the bus reminds one of the advances made in communication networks in the forty-one years which have passed since this view was taken. (A.R.Packer)

During July of the year under review a batch of fifteen RTLs were sent to Northfleet to augment summer services and included RTL1303 which had lain idle and unlicensed at North Street, Romford garage since May 1958. Seen on 5th September with running plates NF37 it is in use on Route 495 to Christianfields Estate. Its Country Area use would terminate some few days later when it was transferred to Hackney garage. (R.A.Golds)

After its March overhaul RTL895 re-entered service garaged at Tottenham, having previously been faithful to Athol Street, Poplar since new in September 1950. With a minimal number of interested passengers it is seen on an excursion to Gatwick Airport in May at a time when Zetters Pools apparently paid £8,000 as a prize for a farthing stake and the Battersea Fun Fair is advertised as open daily from the 9th of the month. (R.A.Golds)

At Aldgate terminus on 21st November Poplar garaged RM102 keeps K1 class trolleybus 1061 of Highgate depot company with a Green Line RT in the far background. All the RM vehicles delivered in the year under review were fitted with bodies which lacked opening front windows to the upper deck and many carried the enigmatic front advertising seen here, the intention of which was to show how this space could be used to target the minds of Joe Public. (W.R.Legg)

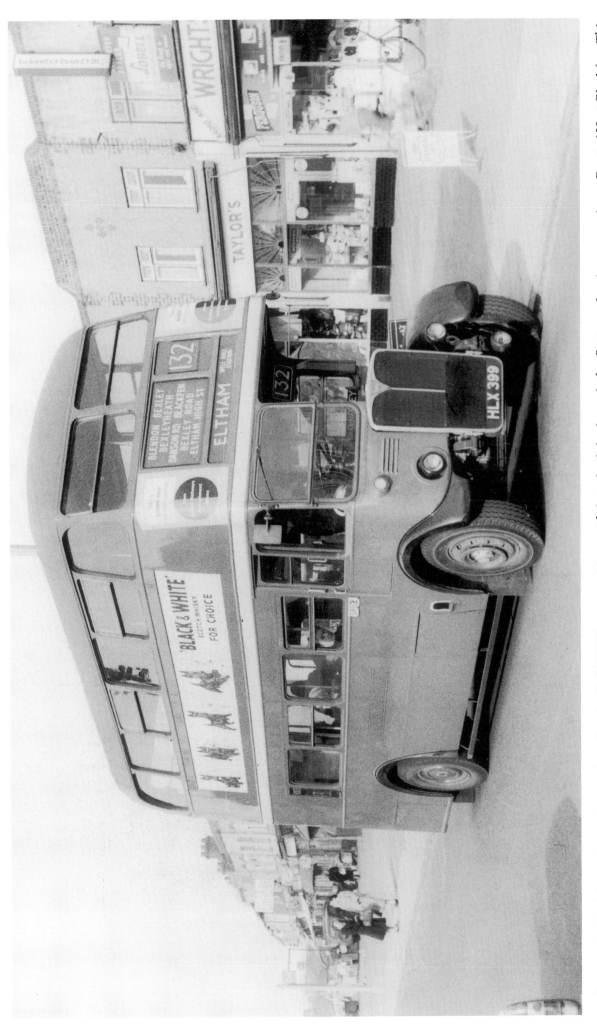

In the 1952 book of this series a picture of roofbox bodied RT582 appears. Now with later built bodywork the fleet number is seen again on Route 132 at Blackfen. This photograph was taken before 4th March, on which date the route lost its circular operation, the section through Bexley village being replaced by new Route 195 in changes connected with the Bexleyheath trolleybus replacement. The 132 gained a Monday to Friday and Saturday afternoon extension to Erith. The unblemished condition of the bodywork is accounted for by the bus having received an overhaul at Aldenham during February of the year under review. (A.Mortimer)

RT2405 waits on the stand at Otter Road, Greenford on 17th January while working Route 55. The destination blind reads 'Chiswick, Swimming Pools', a terminus otherwise known as Chiswick, Edensor Road. Chiswick House mentioned on the bulkhead slipboard was within a short walking distance of the end of the route. The bus, a resident of Southall garage looks very presentable at the halfway stage between overhauls in April 1957 and May 1961. (A.R.Packer)

In the summer of the year under review Clapton garage's RTL1098 on the 277 has pulled into the lay-by at West India Dock which used to be the terminus of the 677 trolleybus that this route replaced on 11th April. The opportunity was taken to extend the replacing bus route down into the Isle of Dogs to Cubitt Town. In the background a short working 567 trolleybus rests without the worry of jockeying for sequence on the wires with the Clapton trolleybuses. In a few months time the wires would go altogether and a Routemaster on 5A would be in its place. (D.A.Ruddom collection)

The entrance shaft of the foot tunnel to Woolwich figures prominently in the background of this busy scene at North Woolwich. Although much redevelopment has taken place at this location that building still remains and offers an alternative to the free ferry ride across the Thames. Passengers alight from RT2672 before it negotiates a U-turn in the wide thoroughfare to take up position for a further journey on Route 101. The trolleybus seen on the departure stand on the far side of the road is on Route 669 to Stratford Broadway which would be replaced by motor bus Route 69 on 3rd February of the following year. (A.R.Packer)

On 24th January Catford's RT349 lays over between runs on the Special Football Service between Grove Park and Charlton Football Ground. One wonders whether the crew has popped into the match while it is in progress. Perhaps some football fan can tell us what match was on at The Valley on that Saturday. In the following month this bus was overhauled and re-appeared from Aldenham carrying similar bodywork, re-entering service at Brixton. (R.A.Golds)

New one person operated Route 399 was introduced on 13th May of the year under review to operate between Bulphan and Rainham via Orsett, Grays and Uplands Estate. On 5th September centrepiece RF578 is seen parked in the Grays garage yard with RT4552 dressed for its regular Green Line duties alongside. Just a few months after its introduction the 399 route changed to crew operation on 14th October still using RFs. (R.A.Golds)

On 1st March RTL337 of Athol Street garage waits at the Crystal Palace terminus before circumnavigating the roundabout at the end of the Parade and returning to Bromley by Bow. Athol Street, Poplar garage, in 1959 the home of an all Leyland allocation of double deck buses, had something of a reprieve as the original plan was for closure with the conversion of nearby Poplar trolleybus depot to a bus garage. As delays mounted in completing facilities at the latter it was not until 1961 that the link with C garage and bus operation through the Thames tunnels stretching back to 1912 was broken. (A.B.Cross)

Standardisation is clearly evident in more ways than one when this line up of RTs is examined more closely. All three are residents of Uxbridge garage and carry identical looking bodywork. Interestingly they carry short working blinds for Route 158 normally worked between Ruislip Lido and Watford Junction by Harrow Weald garage. These buses are obviously scheduled for extras, possibly on a Bank Holiday, at Ruislip between the station and the very popular lido. RT960 parked furthest from the camera is now fitted with the peculiarly London version of direction indicators which the next two, from left to right RT2770 and RT2127 have yet to receive. (R.Wellings)

On 6th March RT3727 heads out of Market Street, Dartford on the last leg of its journey from Chelsfield to Henderson Drive on the then fairly new developments to the north of Dartford. In the background the now defunct trolleybus wires can just be made out on the terminus of the route from Woolwich which is now served by red liveried buses similar to the subject of this photograph. (A.B.Cross)

RT247 stands in lonely isolation at Parsons Hill, Woolwich in between trips on Route 161. This is St.Valentine's Day but the bus seems particularly unloved. The trolleybus in the background has only another two and a half weeks to go before its career will be ended. The low numbered RT served four years in the south east at Sidcup garage. (A.R.Packer)

This nearside picture of RM49 at Walthamstow, Crooked Billet on 17th November shows the bus in use as a learner vehicle from Upton Park and gives a good view of the uncluttered profile of London's latest bus. Note the total lack of polished wheel trim embellishments that followed a cost cutting exercise first introduced in 1956. One of the largest single group of trolleybuses delivered to London Transport and classified as the K class is seen parked on the extreme right. It displays the double-ended blind for short workings on the 685 route. (Bespix)

Donegal Square North in Belfast city centre with former London Transport D13, now fitted with Harkness 56 seat bodywork presents an interesting view. The Belfast Chamber of Commerce offices are to the extreme right of the picture with a further London registered vehicle in the shape of the Royal Mail delivery van parked outside. The only Northern Ireland registered vehicle is the bus in use on Route 78, which carries Belfast County Borough MZ letters. (D.F.Parker)

Twickenham's RT1396 is seen at Butterwick, Hammersmith about to depart on a journey shortened at Richmond Bridge on Sunday Route 90C which, as the intermediate point blind shows, normally reached Staines. The bridge was the destination for buses running into the garage from the north. Originally a Saunders manufactured body carried this fleet number but now a Park Royal product, numbered 3820, has graced the chassis since an overhaul took place in July 1958. (A.R.Packer)

Only the registration DGX272 and a familiar AEC radiator triangle badge give a clue to the ancestry of this pantechnicon bodied furniture van under the railway arches near Fenchurch Street. LPTB 56 seat bodywork had been fitted to the chassis of STL1729 from its entry into service during December 1936 through to its sale in October 1954 to the Salford dealer Lancashire Motor Traders. Subsequently it was converted as seen here but obviously was not treated with much respect, although it managed to remain in use until at least February 1964. (R.H.G.Simpson)

The date is 8th August and RTL349 is seen approaching the northern portal of the Rotherhithe Tunnel on its fairly short journey, which, after a circumnavigation of the Surrey Docks, will end above the southern entrance. The vehicle's period of service at Athol Street, Poplar stretched from its March 1957 overhaul until it was delicensed in October 1960. Put into store at Poplar that month it was eventually disposed of to the Ceylon Transport Board in January of the following year. (J.H.Price)

On a cold but bright 24th January ex-STL1836 is seen with driver in his cab and an eager young child about to board at Peterborough bus station. The vehicle had first entered service in March 1937 as a combination of a 4/9STL chassis to which was mounted a LPTB built STL14 body numbered 17123. In September 1938 it received the STL11 type body number 16911 which it still carries while in the ownership of T.Canham (Services) Ltd. of Whittlesey in a livery of cream with a blue band. It was finally scrapped in March of the following year. (A.R.Packer)

Very presentable RTW121 is halfway through the period between overhauls, having last been attended to in March 1957 with its next visit for similar treatment not taking place until February 1961. It is seen calling into the Butterwick bus station at Hammersmith in April while in service on Route 11 before continuing its journey to Aldwych. A Bedford OB coach gives a period flavour to the view, while one of the B.E.A. 4RF4 coaches is about to enter Butterwick in the distance. (A.R.Packer)

Service trials with the initial deliveries of the new RM class were carried out on a small number of routes with seven garages being involved. Riverside garage received seven of the class for use on Route 11 and here, with the Victoria Palace home of the Crazy Gang in the background, RM37 continues its journey to Shepherds Bush, Wells Road soon after its entry into service. (A.R.Packer)

Route 321A operated along identical roads as its unsuffixed counterpart from Luton to Rickmansworth and then turned off the main road to terminate at the Berry Lane Estate. Seen here journeying to Luton, RT602 had from March of the year under review been garaged in that town's ex-Strawhatter premises, which had a capacity of around twenty-six vehicles. (J.G.S.Smith collection)

RF132 managed to complete its career, which stretched from February 1952 through to December 1964, with London Transport always classified as a 1/2RF2/1, being one of only twenty-four which managed to escape the various modernisation programmes introduced in later years. These two dozen coaches constituted the earliest sales of the class for further use following on the disposal of the Private Hire fleet. At Windsor bus garage sometime in March the coach carries WR77 running plates, which indicates that on the previous day it finished the 'wrong end' of the 718. Therefore this Epping garaged coach is running under Windsor plates. It waits departure for a journey to Harlow New Town via London (Victoria) and Chingford. A 1930s Ford Popular Series Y stands parked in the background. (A.R.Packer)

At St.Mary's Square, Hitchin on 2nd May GS18 lays over before returning to Datchworth on the Tuesday and Saturday market day Route 329A with running plates HG45. Although this GS saw further use from March 1966 to August 1973 with Prowting Holdings Ltd. of Ruislip in Middlesex in a non-p.s.v. capacity, it was eventually scrapped and did not swell the numbers already in the preservation movement by that time. (J.C.Gillham)

RT2252 complete with crew is parked in Gravesend town centre before departure to Dover Road Schools on 21st November. Although delivered in green livery, it entered service at Mortlake garage in July 1949 eventually moving to the Country Area. After its spell at Northfleet garage it would enter Aldenham for overhaul to be outshopped in Green Line livery and take up residence at Swanley Junction garage. It was disposed of to Tillingbourne Valley Services at Guildford in their capacity as a dealer and then mysteriously disappeared, as did most of the members of the class which took this route. (A.R.Packer)

RFW15 stands beside Victoria garage with its blind indicating use on a London Airport Tour. First entering service in June 1951 this AEC Regal IV with Eastern Coach Works bodywork for 39 passengers would eventually be withdrawn from service in October 1963 in the period when London Transport withdrew its entire private hire fleet. The coach was exported to Ceylon in 1964 together with nine of its contemporaries, which left only five of the class still on British soil. Nowadays two of these are privately preserved, the other three having been scrapped. (D.W.K.Jones)

Before its arrival at Tottenham garage in August 1957, RTW339 had operated from Bromley, Willesden and Clay Hall. On 21st March it is seen on the Brookside Road stand at Archway with blinds set in readiness for its Route 41 duty to Tottenham Hale. Note the intermediate point blind allows for the peak hour working through to Ilford. Following its spell at its current garage, it received a final overhaul in May 1961, re-entering service at Chelverton Road, Putney. Subsequently it was transferred to Brixton for its last years of London service before disposal in March 1966. (A.R.Packer)

RLH44 fitted with running plates MA34 stops in Chesham on 27th March on its way to Watford while working Route 336. This particular vehicle was eventually converted into a mobile uniform store by its owners, London Country Bus Services. As 581J it spent over ten years carrying uniforms instead of passengers, finally being sold in January 1983 for preservation. Still preserved in its final condition it makes an unusual and most welcome contribution to the heritage of the British bus scene. (R.A.Golds)

RTL405 en-route for Richmond Bridge on Easter Monday by way of Route 27 is seen at Butterwick, Hammersmith. Since its previous overhaul in May 1957, when it was outshopped from Aldenham Works fitted with body number 9033, Riverside garage has been its home and continued to be so until its last day of passenger use, which occurred in January 1965 at the time Route 27 was converted to RT operation. (A.R.Packer)

Highland Omnibuses Ltd. fleet number K98, registered LSC99, utilises the rebuilt Guy Arab II chassis of an ex-London Transport G class vehicle. Scottish Omnibus Ltd. built the bodywork seating 35 passengers to coach standards in 1954. Unfortunately with the rebuilds carried out during the years 1953 and 1954 by Scottish Motor Traction the original London identification was lost in favour of new chassis numbers SMT1 through to SMT23 which were substituted. Seen here in Inverness Bus Station on 26th July the coach, in its dark red livery, appears to be unwanted for immediate service. Withdrawn in 1966, this hybrid vehicle was despatched to Kelbie, a dealer of Turriff, Grampian, who reduced to scrap a bus whose ancestry could be traced back to the wartime utility years. (A.R.Packer)

Parked outside the 'Brewery Tap' just off the main Barking shopping area, RT3484 waits for a journey to Creekmouth Power Station by way of Route 23C. Not exactly about to pass any worthwhile attraction on its journey, another use has been found for the slipboard on the bulkhead window, which reads 'Hop on a bus'. As to the front advertisement, whether in 1959 the power station workers were the right people for Cooks to target for flight sales is perhaps debatable. (A.R.Packer)

The travelling public always appreciates a clean and well presented means of transport and despite the fact that it is twelve months since its last overhaul, RF659 gives such an appearance. It is waiting to depart from Gravesend on a journey to the White Swan at Ash by way of Route 489 on 5th September. (R.A.Golds)

Much activity takes place around the platform area of RT1016 as it performs duty HH31 on Hemel Hempstead local town service 320 in this January scene. The route was the subject of a small extension to Gadebridge, Galley Hill from 18th February of the year under review. (A.R.Packer)

STL2377, having been in the capable hands of the London Bus Preservation Trust for a number of years, has returned to its former glory in the year 2000. Its last London passenger use had been at Hornchurch garage before withdrawal in March 1954 and sale to North's the Leeds dealer. Mulley's Motorways Ltd. of Ixworth quickly realised it had potential usefulness and after purchase gave it fleet number 39. It first entered the preservation movement in June 1966 and after its recent exhaustive rebuilding programme has joined a very small number of this important class still in existence. (M.A.Sutcliffe)

The fourth stage of the trolleybus replacement programme, the last for the year, took place on 11th November and included the introduction of five new routes. The 238 was run on a Monday to Saturday basis utilising eight RM class vehicles on a Saturday increased by three for the rest of the week. It operated between Chittys Lane at Becontree and Canning Town with an extension to North Woolwich during Monday to Friday peak hours. At the Canning Town terminal on 14th November West Ham garaged RM70 waits to depart for a journey to the eastern terminal. (A.R.Packer)

This most evocative scene at Parsons Hill, Woolwich on Saturday 28th February shows RTs and trolleybuses waiting to take up further duties on their respective routes. RT494, the centrepiece, has a small number of passengers already seated and is to journey as far as Swanley Garage. The full length of the route to Farningham was only served in Monday to Friday peak hours and Saturday shopping times. The trolleybus seen behind the pillar-box is bound for Dartford on Route 696 but next Saturday an RT on Route 96 will be standing in its place. (R.A.Golds)

With B4 running plates RTL1157 is helping out on the Express Service between Morden Station and Epsom Racecourse provided for the summer meeting. Actually allocated at the time to Riverside garage its loan to another garage which housed identical classes broadens its operational use, having only been garaged at Wandsworth and Chalk Farm in earlier years. (A.Mortimer)

RF687 is seen departing Sevenoaks bus station on Saturday 10th January carrying a good load of passengers on Route 413. Converted to its new configuration as a one man operated bus in February 1956, it now seats 39 rather than its original capacity of 41 and is reclassified 2RF5/1 from 2RF2/2. It was scrapped by Booth, the dealer of Rotherham, in November 1975 following its departure from London Country Bus Services Ltd. (A.R.Packer)

RM5, numerically the first production example of a family of vehicles which would number 2760 not including some later acquisitions, is seen working Route 8 in the time it was allocated to Willesden garage. This was from June to November of the year under review. In consequence of the multi-sourcing of electrical, transmission and brake systems for the purpose of obtaining the quality and reliability required by London Transport, numerous sub-classes were built throughout the entire class. In this instance this bus is one of only five built as 5RM5. Is it curiosity or a 'mechanical' that has caused the driver to lift the bonnet? (D.W.K.Jones)

RT3615 with running plates GY11 calls at Grays on Saturday 14th December en-route to Romford from Tilbury Ferry. For the period between its previous overhaul, which took place in March 1956 and its next in September 1960, it was always a resident of Grays garage who operated a network of bus routes in isolation from the rest of the Country Area. (A.R.Packer)

A through journey between Potters Bar and Upshire is nowadays impossible. For a number of years however one could make the trip on an Enfield garaged bus, such as RT782, depicted here on Sunday only Route 242A. This almost rustic scene with a Police public call box, public conveniences and telephone box of the style which is most remembered is on the site where now stands the Waltham Cross Shopping Pavilion. The trolleybus traction pole with its inspector's telephone shows the location to be opposite the trolleybus lay-by. (R.Wellings)

Passengers board RT472 at Acton Town Station just past the entrance to what forty years later would be the London Transport Museum's Depot. The RT3 type bodywork carried still makes use of the nearside corner pillar route plate. Although this combination of chassis and body had received an overhaul in February 1959, the body would be removed in June 1961 after a tree had fallen on it while in service on Route 65. The 265 route shown here had commenced in May 1952 on weekdays between East Acton and Chessington with a Sunday service at the southern end from Kingston. By the time of its demise in December 1966 it had been reduced to a Kingston to Chessington service with Monday to Friday peak workings to Richmond. (A.R.Packer)

The cyclist looks annoyed that anyone should have the effrontery to photograph him in action while doubtless the photographer curses that he has come along just at the wrong moment. Nevertheless it is still an interesting view on 19th May in Slough with RT614 working through to Staines Central Station on the long 441 route from High Wycombe. The RT on Route 484, whose identity is obscured by the said cyclist, appears to be in ex-works condition and looks smart without front advertisements. (A.B.Cross)

RT4526 stands at the damp deserted Larchwood Drive, Englefield Green terminal of the limited stop hospital service 493, which operated from here to Botleys Park, St.Peter's Hospital. Route 441C shown with 493 on the bus stop flag provided the regular service to this point. (R.Wellings)

The bulk of the 10T10 class and its derivatives were disposed of between March 1953 and April 1957, many being immediately scrapped by their new owners. A large number were nevertheless exported while others found further uses as mobile showrooms, staff transport, racing car transporters etc. with at least one being preserved. T600 had been selected for some special purpose after purchase by W.North the dealer of Leeds in May 1953 and was rebuilt at London Transport's Chiswick Works to offside rear door configuration in July. For unknown reasons its further use never materialised and it was left to deteriorate at the Stourton premises of W.North. (K.Lane)

RT1590, a resident of Hornchurch garage, is viewed on 14th February at Rainham waiting its next journey on Route 165 to Clockhouse Lane, Hunters Grove. This route had first appeared on 20th November 1940 using ST class buses for the service, which then operated between Rainham, White Post Corner and Collier Row. The route still continues today but does not venture further north than Romford Market and is in the hands of First Capital. (A.R.Packer)

On 15th July Shepherds Bush garaged RTL1030 stands beside an elderly gas standard which at some time has been adapted to operate with electric power. The bus is working one of the peak hour shuttle journeys from Willesden Junction to Park Royal Stadium. While the route was once one of the longest, although through journeys were rarely, if ever, undertaken, it now only works between Notting Hill Gate and Dulwich in the hands of Go-Ahead group company London Central. (R.A.Golds)

The 423 group of routes provided many local services in Dartford. The 423D was a weekday operation first introduced in 1948 which ran from Watchgate on the south eastern outskirts via the now closed Southern Hospital and the Darenth Park Industrial Training Institution. It then ran into the town along Watling Street and headed south again along the erstwhile spur line of the Dartford tramways to Wilmington Post Office at Barn End Lane. On 14th February RT4120 takes a rest from its labours alongside Dartford garage. (A.R.Packer)

One queue for motor buses and one for trolleybuses appears to be the order of the day with RTL1382 at the head of the former and Class L3 trolleybus 1474 at the other in this view taken at Aldgate Bus Station. Having been delicensed and in store since the previous November, the RTL had re-entered passenger service at Bow garage in August. Route 26 had replaced trolleybus 661 but trolleybus route 567 would last until 10th November. Currently operating from Poplar depot, 1474 would be transferred first to Finchley and later to Fulwell as the dwindling trolleybus system dictated before withdrawal in May 1962 and disposal to George Cohen the following month. (J.A.S.Hambley collection)

Route 468 operated between Epsom and Chessington Zoo via West Ewell, a route which before its suspension during the Second World War was known as 418B - see page 145 of the 1939/45 volume of this series. Leatherhead's RT1014, carrying its last RT3 type body, waits departure time at Epsom railway station on 15th February. Upon its next visit to Aldenham for overhaul body number 8107, originally carried by RT3685, would be outshopped with this fleet number and re-enter service at Hemel Hempstead in the northern Country Area. (A.R.Packer)

RT3149 enters the bus station at Sevenoaks with destination blind already set for the next trip to Heverham by way of Route 421. The sparse via point blind displays the names of the only two villages encountered although Bat & Ball could easily have been included. To the right of the picture an early post-war London taxi passes a quartet of women engaged in conversation and seemingly oblivious of the hazards of moving vehicles. (R.Wellings)

The North Street, Romford crew of Saunders bodied RT469 advance on their charge to take it on the seventy one minute journey to Gooshays Drive at Harold Hill. The 247A only ventured south of Gants Hill to Ilford, where this picture is taken, on a Saturday, doubtless to enhance the service to this popular shopping centre. This particular bus was allocated to North Street from August 1957 through to July 1961. (A.R.Packer)

Three Monday to Friday afternoon journeys on Route 250 were extended from Hornchurch Garage to Corbets Tey on 18th February to restore the service lost with the withdrawal of Route 249 in the previous August. Here TD122 with running plates NS52 waits departure from Epping on the route during the short life of the extension which was withdrawn on 14th April in favour of a new peak hour route 248A. This was identical to the erstwhile 249 but by then that number had been used for a trolleybus replacement route in east London. (R.Wellings)

The 32 route was a sort of hybrid which emerged as a result of the August conversion of the Bow Depot trolleybus routes. It ran on weekdays from Wanstead (not served by trolleybuses) via Leytonstone where it joined the 26 route, which was the 661 replacement, to Stratford from where it also joined with the 25, which had been augmented to replace the 663, and from there boosted the 25 service all the way to Victoria. The trolleybuses of course had ventured no further west than Aldgate. In fact the 32 route only survived until November 1964. Here Bow's RTL1288 passes the Aldgate trolleybus terminus, still used by the J3 class vehicle following it up on the 653. (C.Carter)

Outshopped from an Aldenham overhaul in December 1958, RT479 re-entered service at Norwood garage and is seen here at the Crystal Palace terminal of the weekday Route 137 on 1st March. As was common with the overhaul system then in operation, the body seen here numbered 6954 had originally carried fleet number RT4073. The chassis may also have carried a different RT fleet number as they too swopped identity when going through works with only their 'Chassis Unit' brass plate identifying their original fleet number. (A.B.Cross)

TD104 only spent from November 1958 through to June of the year under review garaged at Uxbridge, being transferred to Edgware with other members of the class upon the conversion of Routes 224, 224A and 224B to RF operation on the 10th of that month. At Uxbridge Underground terminus it waits departure on the unsuffixed service 224 to Laleham on 17th January with RT2868 on Route 198 parked behind the 'Wonderloaf' delivery vehicle. (A.R.Packer)

On the convenient service road adjoining Friday Hill at Chingford Hatch RTL901 lays over before returning to Lower Edmonton, Bounces Road. The running plates, AR2, denote that it is a Saturday on which day Tottenham garage bolstered the Enfield RT allocation on this route with three of their Leyland vehicles. (R.A.Golds)

With a wonderful array of semaphore signals in the far distance, RT4798 stands beside the never to be completed structure of the proposed enlargement of Finsbury Park Station for the intended extension of the Northern City Line over the Alexandra Palace line of the L.N.E.R. The history of this Route 179 can be traced from 6th January 1952 when it was introduced to replace the 74 tram service. Subsequently extended to Finsbury Park in 1958 it would be withdrawn on 7th November 1961 when absorbed into new trolleybus replacement routes 141 and 141A together with a resurrected 4A. The bus had re-entered service after an October 1957 overhaul at New Cross garage where it remained until its next visit to Aldenham in October 1961. (A.R.Packer)

This route 36A lasted almost forty years, having been introduced in connection with stage five of the tram conversion programme in October 1951. It was withdrawn in April 1991 by which time it had been cut back to Victoria from West Kilburn. At Claremont Road, West Kilburn on 15th July Rye Lane garaged RT2029 carries side advertising for what the manufacturers, Invicta, call 'A front briefs', presumably the Kentish pensioner's answer to Y fronts. (R.A.Golds)

Previously an all RT garage, Gillingham Street, Victoria began receiving RTL buses in July from all over the system in a complicated exercise to ensure sufficient RTs would be available at certain East London garages involved in the forthcoming Stage 3 of the trolleybus conversion programme. Wandsworth's RTL1206 was transferred to Gillingham Street in July and is seen at Victoria running round to the station forecourt with destination blind pre-set for a short working to London Bridge on Route 10. (F.W.Ivey)

The familiar bus station at Golders Green provides the temporary refuge for Middle Row's RTL493, while engaged in duties on Route 28 and soon to depart for Wandsworth Bridge. This route can be traced back to July 1911 when it was introduced using B type buses. Initially it ran between Wandsworth Bridge and West Hampstead but three months later it was extended to Golders Green. Only in 1999 did the 28 number disappear from this forecourt. Middle Row's involvement did not happen until 1938 and prior to that Hendon and Battersea had been the main protagonists. (J.Gascoine)

Newly returned to service at Muswell Hill garage from its third overhaul, RT875 on Route 125 has the rudimentary fittings for direction indicators now in place. Beyond, RT1333 on Route 240 with Saunders bodywork still awaits such treatment. Route 125 had first reached this Golders Green Station terminus on 28th November 1951 having previously terminated at Woodside Park, Cissbury Ring South and was the first bus route to run through Frith Lane to Mill Hill East. (R.H.G.Simpson)

This picture caused a few enquiries to be made since it is dated 3rd March 1959. However, RT1238 carries a via point blind for the weekday extension introduced on 4th March as part of the trolleybus conversion of Route 654 whereby the 64 route was extended from West Croydon to Elmers End garage with school journeys to Eden Park. In addition the bus appears to be turning into St.Michael's Road at West Croydon having come from the direction of Elmers End and is bound for the garage at South Croydon. It must be said however that West Croydon seems strangely devoid of traffic for a weekday, even in 1959. (A.B.Cross)

RTL364, a Stockwell resident, is seen at the Crystal Palace terminal on 1st March about to depart on a journey to Golders Green Station by way of Route 2B. This route deviated from the normal service 2 only in that it ran over Tulse Hill rather than continuing along Norwood Road via Herne Hill to Brixton where they both met up once again. With less than eighteen months passenger service remaining this RTL was included in a batch of twenty of the class exported to Ceylon in the first month of 1961. (A.B.Cross)

Route 180, now in its eighth year of existence, was born with Stage 5 of the tram conversion programme on 7th October 1951. Catford garage remained the operating base for the route although RT3685 only reached the garage during May 1956 upon its return from its first overhaul. Seen at Parsons Hill, Woolwich on 4th March it waits departure to Lower Sydenham Station with another RT about to negotiate the road junction with newly defunct trolleybus wiring sweeping round the corner. (A.R.Packer)

Two of the first generation of the RT class together with a Triumph 'Mayflower' car stand on the approach road to West Ham trolleybus depot. RT83 nearest the camera has lost its London Transport triangle at the top of the radiator and sustained some damage on its nearside. RT134 in the distance looks in much better condition. During this period of time the 2RT2 was the mainstay of the double deck learner fleet and when finally withdrawn they were replaced by post-war RT family vehicles. These two RTs left the capital in March 1963 and January 1961 respectively. (F.W.Ivey)

Route 100 was worked by buses off Route 15 and RTW78 stands at the East Ham, 'White Horse' terminal presumably ready to run 'dead' to Barking for its stint on the 100. The canopy blind reads '15' and probably will not be changed and the slipboard 'To and From the National Gallery' will remain incongruously in place. Seven Kings garaged RT913, soon to depart for Lambourne End on Route 150, stands alongside in this Sunday view. (A.Mortimer)

No trolleybuses are in evidence in this 30th March view at Butterwick, Hammersmith although they certainly were still in operation and their depot can be seen adjacent to the roadway. RTL1432 in service on Route 72 continues its journey to Roehampton. In April 1958 it joined many similar vehicles then garaged at Riverside which also housed some RTW class buses until changes in far off 1966 saw the introduction of the RT and RM classes to this base. (A.R.Packer)

Peterborough was worth a visit in 1959, if only for the number of former STLs that could be seen. On 30th May ex-STL896, withdrawn and sold by London Transport in the summer of 1953 is now in the ownership of its second operator, having previously been the property of Longlands (Crowland) Ltd. who traded as Grey Green Bus. Since December 1958 it has been operated by J.R.Morley & Sons Ltd. of Whittlesey in a grey and red colour scheme but sadly would be scrapped two years after purchase. (A.R.Packer)

On Saturday 7th February and carrying an appreciable number of passengers, RT3598 with SA37 running plates heads into St.Albans along Catherine Street on Route 343 displaying the localised destination 'St.Peters Street L.T.Garage'. In addition to short journeys such as this the 343 provided a through 30-minute service on Saturdays between Dunstable Square and Brookmans Park Station. The bus was garaged at St.Albans between overhauls in February 1956 and July 1960. (A.R.Packer)

With the solid edifice of Windsor garage as a background, RT3635 stands ready for service on Route 417 from Windsor to Langley Village sometime in March. The lower panel mouldings are beginning to show signs of wear although it is still a further year before an overhaul will be carried out on the bus. (A.R.Packer)

All-Leyland, Willesden garaged RTW3 waits at Edgware Station before departure on Route 18 to Wembley, Empire Pool having attracted at least one female passenger. Just what the gentleman at the stop is waiting for is not clear. In the far background non-roof box RT4760 of Harrow Weald garage is of interest in being the highest numbered Weymann bodied red liveried example delivered to London Transport. The RT3 bodied RT1381 furthest from the camera is also from the same garage. (J.G.S.Smith collection)

The sun was certainly not in evidence on this particular August day when ex-STL1739 was photographed at Peterborough. Owned by T.Canham (Services) Ltd. of Whittlesey, Cambridgeshire from November 1953 until it was scrapped in May 1960, it is clear that almost no changes have been made to its exterior, save for the removal of the running plate bracketry. (M.A.Sutcliffe)

An interesting comparison in the development of single deck bus design is provided by this view of an RF of 1952 and a Q of 1935 at Manor House. CGJ180, now Mobile Gas Unit 1035CD, originally entered service in October 1935 as Country Area bus Q75. To the left of the picture RF216 had initially entered service in April 1952 and now works the long haul of Green Line Route 718 from Harlow to Windsor. The Q on the other hand has probably only journeyed from its base at Tottenham garage. (F.W.Ivey)

RT3886 stands at the terminus of Route 353 at Berkhamsted Station alongside the substantial viaduct of the first main line railway to reach London - the London and Birmingham. On the other side of the railway are the remains of the Norman Berkhamsted Castle, part of which was destroyed in 1838 when the railway was first built. Doubtless today wiser counsels would have ensured its protection. This is the 30th January and the Amersham garaged bus waits to travel through the attractive Chiltern countryside on its way to Windsor. (A.R.Packer)

One of the slave rigs was shown in the 1958 volume of this series of books simulating Route 11. Here an example of these very odd looking vehicles is seen at Victoria Station apparently shadowing a Route 52 bus. Originally Riverside and Willesden garage had the honour of housing the two mobile test beds for use on roads covered by Routes 11 and 46 respectively although here it would seem that Willesden have ventured their example on to a different route. Later they both moved, one to Battersea and the other to Tottenham continuing their evaluation work on Routes 22 and 76 respectively. By early 1960 both unit sets had been re-bodied to enter service later as RM341 and RM398. (W.R.Legg)

RT94 in its learner role stands beside Amersham garage on 3rd January before another journey at the hands of a novice driver. It is eight years since it was last used in public service and its general appearance is beginning to deteriorate. However, it must face another four years performing this arduous task before its final demise. (A.R.Packer)

RM2 negotiates Queen Caroline Street, Hammersmith partly obscured by two cars, a Wolseley 1500 nearest the camera and a Ford Consul. The Turnham Green allocation on Route 91 had for many years been used by the experimental department at nearby Chiswick Works for the evaluation in service of experimental vehicles, hence RM2's presence. The two trolleybuses, which lack blinds, are B1s making their way from Carshalton Depot to meet their fate at the hands of George Cohen in his scrapyard at Colindale. (M.Dryhurst)

RT1001 leaves the bus stop outside St. Albans garage on the circular route 354 which emanated from Chestnut Drive at Marshalswick and looped via Fleetville and the City centre. Although sometimes sparse in blind details, in 1959 this clear display is very pleasing. The bus, a normal resident of Hatfield garage, was never officially allocated to St. Albans but in this view is on loan and carries SA40 running plates. (A.R.Packer)

Standing in the Station Approach at Leatherhead, RF636 has arrived from Boxhill on Route 422. A Southern Region 4-SUB unit painted in the traditional Southern green livery is perched on the embankment behind and it is interesting to notice the absence of any yellow paint on the cab end. (A.R.Packer)

Parked within the St. Albans garage yard on 7th February the blind display on RT3169 appears to be a little awry. It would seem to be working the Saturday shuttle service between St.Albans and Sheephouse Farm Estate at London Colney, which in 1959 was numbered as 358. The side and canopy blinds acknowledge this but the front number blind shows 338, which was the route from which the 358 allocation was derived. (A.R.Packer)

RT1018 lays over on its stand at Slough Station on 18th October before departing on a short journey on the 460 to Datchet, London Road North, rather than covering the full service through to Staines. The RT3 bodywork seen here was discarded in favour of an RT8 example upon overhaul in April 1960. It subsequently continued in service until September 1977 with further use as a training vehicle through to March 1981 when it was obtained for preservation. (P.J.Malsher)

RTL1482 with RTL392 is seen standing outside Athol Street garage, Poplar in an area which still shows the open spaces of wartime damage. The lead RTL carries route information for the Special Dock Service operated between Custom House and Manor Way (Royal Albert Dock) which through its long life was never given a number. While the front vehicle has gained its trafficator 'ears', the one behind has yet to receive this enhancement. (F.W.Ivey)

One of the landmark buildings of Kingston upon Thames, the Empire Theatre now sadly in use as a supermarket, towers in the background behind RT3104 which has commenced a journey to Walton on Thames from the nearby railway station forecourt on 16th May. In the years between its previous overhaul of October 1957 and its next taking place in October 1961 the bus would perform on Norbiton garage's double deck routes 65, 85, 131 and 265 and in its last couple of months at the south west London garage could have made an appearance in Central London on the Sunday 14 allocation. (A.B.Cross)

A conductress, moneybag over her shoulder and the all important timecard in hand, approaches the time clock mounted on the brickwork of the Piccadilly Line Cockfosters station. Engaged on Route 29, this procedure would be required of all crews en-route to the southern terminals including Victoria. From the angle of her approach it would suggest that she has conversed with the driver to while away the time he has picked up on the journey so far from South Mimms. RT4065 being a Potters Bar bus working through to Victoria, confirms this picture must have been taken on a Sunday or Bank Holiday. Standing proud above the station, the bullseye totems proclaim the station's name and owners. (M.Rooum)

Still fitted with an unspoilt rear wheel cover, or 'dustbin lid' as they were often called, RT90 negotiates road works involved with the flyover construction for the M4 motorway at Chiswick. This bus had commenced its service on Route 14 in May 1940 garaged at Putney Bridge, having been taken into stock in mid-March of the same year. Its last eight years in the ownership of London Transport were spent firstly as a staff bus and later in the role of a learner vehicle before disposal to George Cohen for scrapping in September 1963. (R.H.G.Simpson)

Route 375 would be converted to RF one-man operation and withdrawn between White Post Corner and the War Memorial at Rainham with the Country Bus changes introduced on 13th May. This was followed by total withdrawal on 30th June. Earlier in the year T788 stands at Rainham Church representing the class in their last months of operation from Grays garage. The replacement RFs were also to depart the garage during October leaving an allocation consisting solely of RTs. (A.R.Packer)

Overhauled the previous year, RTL688 had re-entered service at Walworth garage but after three months returned to Camberwell which had been its home since its first day of service in March 1950. Devoid of a side advertisement it is seen on 13th January at the Embankment, Horse Guards Avenue terminus before a journey on Route 168 to Putney Heath, Green Man. (R.A.Golds)

Passengers disembark from RLH74 at North Harrow Station, Imperial Drive on 25th August with no one remaining for the final mile of its journey on Route 230 to Rayners Lane Station. Initially entering service at Merton garage in December 1952, it was transferred to Harrow Weald in November 1956 where it remained until withdrawal from service in June 1969. (J.C.Gillham)

Buses on two new routes introduced with the Bexleyheath trolleybus conversion scheme implemented on 4th March are shown in this scene at Woolwich on the first day of the new order. The lead vehicle, RT3068 with running plates AW1, contributes to Route 177A which required three buses on Monday to Saturday. An unidentifiable RT garaged at Bexleyheath is parked furthest from the camera on Route 195 which used sixteen buses on Saturdays with less at other times. Both routes were relatively short-lived being withdrawn in May 1963. (A.R.Packer)

RM71 is seen at the rush hour only terminus of Route 238 at North Woolwich, being one of five of the class provided by Poplar garage on a Monday to Friday basis for the route. The former trolleybus driver will no longer have a need for the bamboo pole hanging on the trolleybus standard at the rear, although he will still need care in negotiating the slippery looking cobbles. The inspector - a breed now almost extinct - may be about to point out that a change of destination blind is required before departure. (A.Mortimer)

Under trolleybus wires in Goswell Road, RT2602 journeys south to Grove Park. It is April and the lack of traffic suggests a Sunday. The overhead wires will cease to be used after the 15th when Route 677 is withdrawn. The bus had been overhauled in February and remained at New Cross until May 1961 when it moved to Sutton. (A.R.Packer)

TD67 was withdrawn in June of the year under review to be exported to Ceylon. Last overhauled in September 1955, it is seen in its final months of passenger use with London Transport as it waits departure on a short journey to Mill Hill Broadway from the Edgware Station forecourt. (A.Mortimer)

Sometime during sunny May RT3278 rests at the Royal Forest Hotel, Chingford before commencing a journey to Victoria on Route 38 with running plates T2. Prior to being transferred to Leyton earlier in the month the bus had completed a few days passenger service in the unfamiliar territory of the Country Area, being garaged at Grays. The array of 'dolly stops' in front of the mobile canteen are in readiness for Bank Holiday and Sunday use when, due to the number of passengers and the fact that some buses went further on into Epping Forest, passenger loading was transferred to the opposite side of the road. (R.A.Golds)

TD58 with TD110 behind carry running plates NB1 and NB2 respectively on 10th May for what appears to be a rail replacement service on the Southern Region. Most seats are now occupied with passengers impatient for departure. The lamppost on the platform above carries a lozenge station nameplate and a stop sign for 4-car trains. (J.H.Aston)

RT621 heads down Watford High Street on its way to the village of Shenley via Bushey and Radlett. This revised design RT3 bodied bus would continue to be based at Watford High Street until transfer to Amersham in April of the year under review when the former garage closed. (R.A.Golds)

Craven bodied RT1490 had been disposed of to Bird's Commercial Motors in April 1957 and was acquired by Cunningham's Bus Services of Paisley before the year end. Treated to a little cosmetic surgery, it was soon in regular passenger service with its new operator's fleet number 21, being renumbered 29 later in life. A large number of these RTs which were disposed of quite early and purchased by smaller operators, managed roughly five or six years further service before being scrapped. The lack of heavy maintenance facilities prevented them being maintained to the increasingly stringent standards required by legislation. (J.A.S.Hambley collection)

Loughton garaged RT1195 is seen at Ilford waiting to journey to Debden on Route 167 with running plates L70. This fleet number was only involved in two overhauls before spending its last years of service garaged at Enfield and was eventually sold in January 1964 to Bird's Commercial Motors. Oddly it never found a buyer but was allowed to deteriorate at the dealer's Long Marston premises. (A.R.Packer)

A clever piece of parking in Colindale trolleybus depot has been performed by the staff responsible for this tightly packed line up of withdrawn TD class vehicles. From left to right TD63, 64, 73, 67 and 49 wait movement to the docks for shipment to Ceylon. The two gentlemen were perhaps those involved with the parking. They certainly look self-satisfied and one enjoys a cigarette, which might raise the hackles of a present day Health and Safety Officer. (J.A.S.Hambley collection)

Ex-RTL33, which at this date comprises the chassis which first bore fleet number RTL1387 and body number 2222, first carried by RTL9, is now in the ownership of O.K.Motor Services Ltd. (W.Emmerson) of Bishop Auckland in County Durham. It had been acquired via the dealer Birds of Stratford-upon-Avon in March 1958. Now resplendent in its new operator's colour scheme of maroon, red and cream it waits further use at West Auckland lacking any fleet number with the registration being considered sufficient means of identification. Departing the fleet in 1970 it was then scrapped by Morley, a dealer of the nearby town of Shildon. (A.Mortimer)

RT3859 received an overhaul in February, reappearing in Central Area livery having previously been in Country Area colours at Windsor and Swanley Junction since new in September 1950. In pristine condition it is seen at Parsons Hill, Woolwich on 4th March soon to depart for Eltham, Well Hall Station via new route 195 on its first day of operation. The bowstring traction support and trolley-bus wires have become redundant overnight and no more 696s or 698s will be seen at this terminus. (A.R.Packer)

A badly tensioned via blind is fitted to RT1531 seen parked at the Old Town terminal at Clapham Common in sunny August weather. With the return of normal working after the disastrous 1958 strike the earlier service numbered 189 had been withdrawn as part of the first Central Area bus cuts introduced on 20th August. The route number was again in use with the third stage of route alterations which were implemented in the week commencing 26th November when the old 189A was renumbered into the vacant parent number. A neat Morris 10, circa 1934, is parked beneath the double-headed lamppost with another Merton garaged bus positioned closely behind the subject of the photograph. (R.A.Golds)

The low route number 5 was conveniently vacant at the time of the Stage 4 of the trolleybus conversion programme on 11th November and was a useful replacement for the 665 trolleybus route. Delivered to Aldenham from Park Royal Vehicles in September, RM72 was moved later in the month to Poplar depot to await its entry into public service. It helped inaugurate the conversion which required 71 of these new machines on Monday to Friday, dropping to 58 on Saturday with a further drop to 40 for Sunday working. Here, three days after entry into service, it heads east to Barking garage. (A.R.Packer)

Three roof box fitted RTs, albeit not all RT3 bodied stand in line at Forest Hill and present a handsome sight. The lead bus, Elmers End garaged RT297 with Weymann bodywork of the earliest post-war type, waits to depart for Croydon Airport on a Route 194 working, while following Saunders bodied RT1212 will journey to Eltham on Route 124. Another RT3 bodied example completes the trio while mention must be made of the rare Hillman Minx drop-head coupé parked on the opposite side of the thoroughfare. (J.Gascoine)

D179 started life in passenger service in March 1946 from London Road, Romford garage to be withdrawn from its London sphere of operations in February 1953 at which time it was garaged at Merton. Disposed of to W.North & Sons of Leeds the following month it then passed to Brown's Blue, an operator of Markfield, Leicestershire a further month on. It is seen in August of the year under review at the operator's premises being prepared for its final journey to the scrapyard at Stratford-upon-Avon later in the month, having been out of use since the previous February. (M.A.Sutcliffe)

Prior to the conversion of the 224 group of routes from TD to RF operation at Uxbridge garage, Mann Egerton bodied TD103 is seen at Uxbridge Station on 17th January. It is working the 224B route to West Drayton, Stockley Estate, which in 1959 had not yet developed into the business area found there today. The 'Hop on a Bus' slipboard and roof cantrail advert were part of the contemporary effort at encouraging bus travel. (A.R.Packer)

RLH43 is seen in the summer near Biggin Hill as it journeys to Bromley North Station on Route 410. After a spell at East Grinstead the bus was transferred to Godstone in February 1955 where it remained until August 1960, apart from a period in the Central Area at Harrow Weald. It ended its passenger service with London Transport at Addlestone in October 1964. (A.Mortimer)

On 16th May RT4403 in service on Route 90B is about to be overtaken in Twickenham by a London Austin taxi and both are pursued by a trolleybus in service on Route 601. When it first entered service in October 1953 garaged at Merton the RT carried the body first mounted on the chassis of SRT48 but at the time of its first overhaul in March 1957 this was replaced. With its next visit to Aldenham in April 1961 the bus re-entered service in Country Area livery, only to return to its original livery at the time of its third visit in November 1965. (A.B.Cross)

RT2175 waits departure from Woolwich on 4th March to journey to Erith on Route 122A which was introduced on 21st February 1951 to serve the Bedonwell Road area to the north east of Long Lane. A long time survivor of the class this RT fleet number eventually succumbed to the breaker's torch in February 1976 with the Wombwell Diesels Company. (A.R.Packer)

The eight feet wide Duple Midland (Nudd) 55 seat bodywork built in 1952 hides the Guy Arab Mark II chassis of 1945 manufacture on which it is mounted so well that the ordinary travelling public could never guess its former condition. G205 had originally entered service at Hornchurch garage with Park Royal 56-seat bodywork in September 1945 in a brown and yellow ochre livery with pinkish-brown roof. Now in maroon and white and in the ownership of Edinburgh Corporation as their fleet number 337, it carries a May 1952 Edinburgh registration, JWS617, and is seen in the City Centre on 23rd July. The bus with full fronted bodywork managed fifteen years of passenger service compared to only a little over five with its original bodywork. (A.R.Packer)

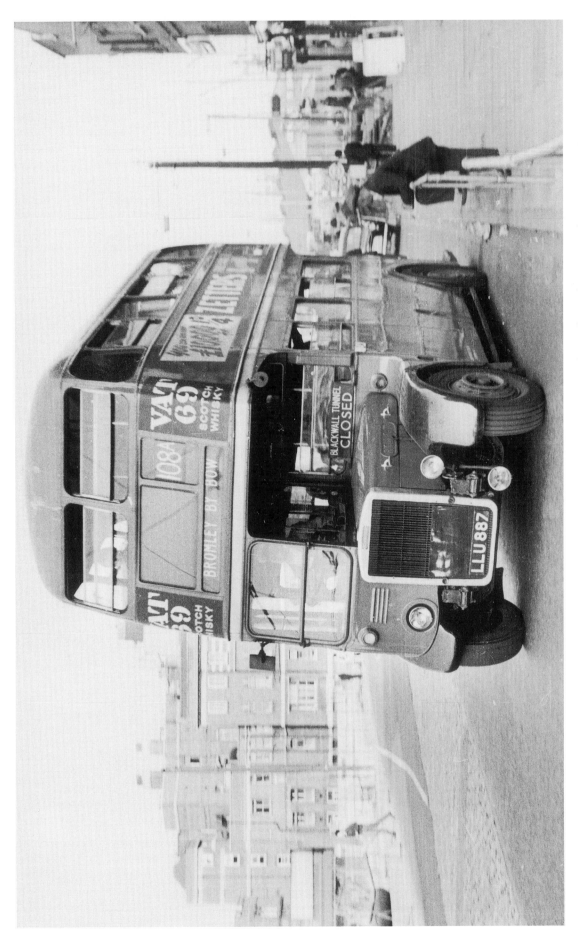

RTL897 carries a slipboard announcing the closure of Blackwall Tunnel, a common occurrence throughout the years when maintenance work or accidents have to be attended to. The board does not offer advice but on such occasions through buses made the long diversion via either Rotherhithe Tunnel, Tower Bridge or even London Bridge but the blank via point blind and location on East India Dock Road of this bus suggests it may be working a simple shuttle between here and Bromley by Bow. The bus had re-entered service at Athol Street, Poplar garage after an overhaul in March and completed almost eighteen months use back and forth under the River Thames before transfer to Bow garage in October 1960. (A.Mortimer)

RTL1224 is seen with running plates AC8 at the Wembley, Empire Pool with the Wembley lion apparently standing on its roof. The blind has yet to be set for the return journey to Edgware on this Park Royal bodied bus which dates from May 1951. In July the vehicle would be transferred to Gillingham Street, Victoria as part of an ongoing programme to rid the centrally placed garage of its RTs in preference to RTLs. (A.R.Packer)

Belfast Corporation number 483, a Daimler CWA6 with Harkness bodywork traverses the wide thoroughfare of Donegal Square North with two sets of trolleybus wiring on the nearside. The bus, which utilises the chassis of ex-D124 is in use on Route 76 to Gilnahirk via Albert Bridge. Originally entering service in August 1945 with Brush bodywork, it was to operate in its original condition for over two years in Belfast before being rebodied in 1956. Finally withdrawn from service in May 1970 it was disposed of to J.Megoran, a dealer of Ballynahinch for scrap. (D.F.Parker)

With the fourth stage of the trolleybus replacement programme on 11th November, four new daytime and one night route were introduced with extensions to various other established services. The only motor bus route which was withdrawn at the time was the 23B, which at its fullest operated between Chittys Lane at Becontree and the Thames View Estate. The main service between Barking, Blake's Corner and Thames View Estate, on which RT2408 is working in this picture, was covered by an extension of the 193 route. This Park Royal bodied RT's two year use at Barking garage came to an end when it entered Aldenham for its third overhaul, re-entering service in October 1960 at nearby North Street, Romford. (A.R.Packer)

TD35 is seen at Hampton Court Station with throngs of visitors making their way to the road bridge and their final destination on the further side of the River Thames. A pre-war Citroen car with driver clearly visible waits for the bus to move forward and a hand signal from the on-duty policeman whose job is temporarily impeded by the same intruder on to the station forecourt. The blind displayed indicates a short working to Esher but the via points are those intended for garage workings on to the route from Kingston. (R.Wellings)

The long awaited delivery of the RM class started during the summer of the year now under review and their entry into service was initially on a trial basis. RM35, one of a small number garaged at Cricklewood, is seen completing a journey from Golders Green Station on Route 2 at Vauxhall Bridge Road, Victoria sometime during August. This route of course had previously seen Routemaster operation in 1956 when RM1 made its debut. (A.R.Packer)

A fairly complicated overhead wiring system at Gardiner's Corner, Whitechapel High Street straddles ex-STD78 as it traverses the wide junction by Aldgate East Station. The Hamsters Mobile Theatre Group used the bus for a number of years and here it carries advertising for their latest presentation 'The Schoolmistress'. Presumably this is a Sunday or Bank Holiday afternoon since an enterprising young gentleman is using the doorway of the closed Woolworth store to sell his wares. (J.Gascoine collection)

Upon its re-entry into service following overhaul in July, RT3339 was garaged at Edgware. It is seen in Kensington Road en-route for Borehamwood, Rossington Avenue on the Sunday extension of Route 52, which was the only time the north-west London garage's vehicles ventured into inner London. The RT3 type bodywork fitted, numbered 1970, first carried the fleet number RT691 and it is noteworthy that a correct route number plate is fitted to the nearside corner pillar holder at this late date. After its passenger service at Edgware, the bus would be delicensed in July 1964 to await disposal which followed in the November. The policemen appear to be interested in happenings further along the road and their call box is handily situated if they need to contact the station. (K.Lane)

Norwood garage officially only operated the RT class bus during the years 1950 through to 1966. So just why RTL985 with running plates N23 should be performing an 'EXTRA' duty on Route 3 is at present an unsolved mystery. It is seen at Crystal Palace terminal waiting departure on a shortened journey as far as Charing Cross rather than the full service through to Camden Town. (A.B.Cross)

A short working only as far as Wexham Street on Route 335 from the terminal at Windsor bus station sometime during March will assure that RT3180 is back at its garage much sooner than if it was covering the full service through to Watford. By contrast the Green Line RF alongside has a much lengthier journey on Route 718 before passing its home garage of Epping on the way to Harlow New Town. (A.R.Packer)

Winter sunshine in Rennell Street, Lewisham on 3rd January brightens up RT4133 and the driver peers behind, no doubt urging the heavily laden passenger to board so that he can depart. He might have usefully filled the time by changing his destination blind, which should probably be showing Welling. This bus would sever all links with New Cross garage when it entered Aldenham in April for overhaul, re-entering service at Norwood. (R.A.Golds)

While carrying two identical notices exhorting boarders to 'pay as you enter - fares ready please', RF695 arrives in Guildford well laden and now nearing the end of a journey on Route 425 from Dorking. A 'To and from Guildford Market' slipboard is carried beneath the first saloon window, which suggests that the service on this occasion was used primarily by shoppers rather than visitors to the various interesting places passed en-route. (R.Stanmore)

Until April Route 38A operated along the roads of its unsuffixed counterpart from Victoria, the routes eventually parting company at Baker's Arms, Leyton to continue to their respective destinations. However, after 11th April Route 38A was used to replace trolleybus 581, which almost paralleled it from Bloomsbury to Woodford. On that date 38A was diverted via Graham Road at Hackney following the erstwhile trolleybus wires, while the 38 continued to run via Pembury Road. RT229 is seen at Victoria Station before departure to Loughton Station. It had re-entered service from its last overhaul in September 1958 garaged at Loughton and was to be delicensed in February 1963 to await disposal, which took place in January 1964. (A.R.Packer)

Country Area bus RF685 deputises for a coach on Green Line Route 714 with LS55 running plates. The recent fall of snow gives Park Lane and Hyde Park a very wintry aspect. The seats on the bus are not as comfortable for long distance passengers as they might be and there are no luggage racks on which to put bags but at least a vehicle has been provided. (A.Mortimer)

Bonnet number RT1152 is best remembered as that carried by the first RT3/3 body built by the Saunders Engineering and Shipyard Company Ltd. of Beaumaris, entering passenger service in January 1949. Outwardly the bodywork closely followed the lines of the RT3 product manufactured in earlier years by Park Royal and Weymann with the one obvious exception being that the offside route number plate holder was centrally placed in the last panel. Beneath the surface however considerable differences existed. The crew in the lower saloon converse prior to another journey from Kings Cross on Route 63 to Honor Oak, Forest Hill Tavern on Sunday 22nd March. (A.R.Packer)

Ex-RT159 still carries its London fleet number, colour scheme and offside 'route' panel fixture although the two panels which once carried the legend 'London Transport' have been repainted. It is only the Jackson display fitted to the front blind boxes, which confirms that the bus is now in the ownership of its second operator with premises in Castle Bromwich. Eventually H.Evans, a dealer in Worsborough Dale, South Derbyshire scrapped the bus in April 1965. (A.Mortimer)

In the green and cream livery of Longlands of Crowland, Lincolnshire, ex-RT1514 is viewed at Peterborough with steamed up upper deck windows in this scene taken on a cold 21st January. As with many disposed Craven bodied RTs the roof box has been removed and an AEC radiator badge substituted for the original London Transport variety. The following year the bus was in the ownership of Mulley's Motorways of Ixworth, Suffolk before eventually being noted in May 1975 on the premises of Piper trading as Hillside Autos, a dealer of Great Yeldham. (A.R.Packer)

Ex-G293 in Alexander & Sons Ltd. maroon livery looks very imposing parked in the Perth garage yard on 24th July having just been outshopped after repaint. The N.C.M.E. bodywork has had the front route aperture rebuilt to Alexander's standard and though no other external modifications have been carried out the colour change gives the bus a very different appearance to when it originally entered service in London in the last month of 1945. Eventually withdrawn from service in 1962 it passed through the hands of the dealer Milburn Motors of Glasgow before meeting its final fate at the premises of Dunsmore, a dealer of Larkhall. (A.R.Packer)

Standing at Willesden during August RM28 appears to have attracted two young bus spotters who have logged their surprise visitor on the Sunday and Bank Holiday route 8B. The body carried by this vehicle incorporates the separate air scoops for ventilation above the upper deck windows and is of 4/5RM5/4 classification. Later in the year it was delicensed, not being used in revenue earning capacity again until the following year when West Ham became its new home. (A.R.Packer)

Ex-G150 had already completed five and a half years passenger service with W.S.Rowbotham of Harriseahead, Staffs. before the Potteries Motor Traction Co.Ltd. acquired the business in January of the year under review. In its new owner's livery and carrying fleet number H470 it is seen still in operation in the territory to which it had grown accustomed in the past six years. Unimpressed with its qualities PMT sold the Park Royal bodied Guy Arab for scrap to the dealer F.Cowley of Salford in November 1960. (J.A.S.Hambley collection)

RT2595 cruises down the gentle slope of Haymarket with the Theatre Royal in the background as it continues a journey to Crystal Palace on route 3 which probably started at Camden Town. The original RT8 type body carried has found a further chassis as its carrier while an earlier style RT3 body is now fitted and would suffice the remaining years of service even after its export to South Africa in July 1964. A Morris Minor Traveller follows behind the bus. (K.Lane)

RM66 leaves the premises of Park Royal Vehicles Ltd. for delivery to London Transport on a sunny day sometime during October. Before delivery to Poplar garage route blinds would be fitted and advertisements pasted on. The fact that this latter task was done centrally deprived us of the pleasure of seeing brand new unadorned Routemasters in service. Elsewhere in this book this RM can be seen just after it entered service. (F.W.Ivey)

RM49 occupies the time-honoured stand for Route 76 in Victoria Station forecourt during its short stay garaged at Tottenham from September to November of the year under review. Tottenham's six RMs at this period were used on Routes 34B and 76 in the so-called pre-service trials. Further to the right RT2940 seems to have been pulled off the Route 16 stand for some reason although the blind is still set for Cricklewood (Crown). (R.Wellings)

On Saturday 10th January at Orpington Station RT2863 gathers intending passengers on its journey from Bromley to Eltham, Well Hall Station over Route 61. In the distance a long time resident of Dunton Green garage, GS23, collects its clients for the circular run on Route 471. Four years later the RT would change its colour scheme to that worn by the GS and initially be garaged at St.Albans. (A.R.Packer)

Until 1st March of the year under review special Sunday services between Eltham, Well Hall Station and Bexley Hospital were provided as a bifurcation on Route 132 running with a blank via blind to avoid confusion with buses running the full circle. After that Sunday when the route lost its Bexley Village section, the task was performed by an extension of Route 124. RT833 demonstrates the 132 working at Well Hall Station having attracted several passengers who, from the seats they have chosen, appear likely to be making the full journey to visit their sick relatives or friends. (R.Wellings)

With the entrance to the Royal Mews as a background, RT1541 rests on the stand at Windsor in company with a Country Area RT before both depart for the High Street to commence their respective journeys. On its next but one visit to Aldenham Works for overhaul, the Central Area liveried RT would join the ranks of the green painted examples being garaged at Hatfield, where the fleet number always appeared a little unusual. (A.R.Packer)

Representatives of the varied fleet operated by A.H.Kearsey and Son of Cheltenham in 1959 are seen in this line-up parked upon their premises. To the extreme left of the picture, with rebuilt windows and having lost its destination equipment, is Brush bodied former D101 of 1945 manufacture. The handsome looking double deck standing next in line last ran for London Transport as RTL149 but is actually the chassis of the original RTL129 and the body which first carried fleet number RTL62. Furthest from the camera, although not of particular interest to the London enthusiast, is a Leyland coach with full fronted body. (R.Wellings)

The variety of advertising carried by the London bus is clearly evident in this line up of vehicles at Barking. RT659 heading the queue had been transferred to Barking from Gillingham Street, Victoria during August and now performs on new bus route 169 which was the replacement for trolleybus service 691 on 19th August. (A.R.Packer)

Spring sunshine and warmth allows saloon windows to be open on RT4613 as it pulls away from the stop outside Enfield garage at Ponders End on its way to Enfield Chase Station on Route 107A. The trolleybus wiring of the Ponders End terminus casts its shadows in angled fashion on the Weymann bodywork now in place on the bus. This fleet number became well known when, in 1978, the then owners, The Vintage Bus Company, rebuilt the body to represent an earlier era of transport operation. Half a side window's width to the upper deck was removed at the front and rear, while the staircase was rebuilt to an open configuration resulting in a clumsy looking vintage appearance which may have fooled some tourists. (R.A.Golds)

On a wet Saturday in February RF675 takes on some bedraggled shoppers in Leatherhead while working a Route 416 journey to Tadworth Station. Once the province of RTs (and even RTC1 at one time), two RFs are now sufficient to meet the service demand between Esher and Tadworth. (A.R.Packer)

Ex-RT204 in its new striking livery of the Tollesbury operator, G.W.Osborne & Sons, arrives at the Colchester bus station on 18th July with a respectable load of passengers and the conductor standing on the platform. This bus had been one of a pair disposed of by London Transport in December of the previous year. The other, RT213, entered service with Cunningham's Bus Services. RT204 had entered service initially in October 1947 and compares favourably with the pre-war Leyland Tiger TS coach owned by Norfolk's of Nayland seen resting in the background. After twenty year's passenger service the AEC Regent MkIII with Park Royal bodywork would be reduced to scrap at the hands of the Basildon Salvage Company some years before the last of the class would be withdrawn from service in the capital. (J.A.S.Hambley collection)

The B.O.A.C. Airways building proudly displays the company logo as RFW10 leads RFW15 along Buckingham Palace Road past the entrance to Victoria coach station, which is to the right of the photographer. Both coaches had received an overhaul in 1956 having initially entered service nearly five years earlier and were to receive a further overhaul before their untimely demise from the fleet. (D.F.Parker)

Opposite the rear of Willesden garage in Pound Lane, New Cross garaged RT1910 waits to journey to Lewisham by way of Route 1, while parked further along the road are an RTW and RML3. The RT carries Weymann body number 1800, which was first fitted to the chassis of RT551. Mounted on this RT since May 1958 when it re-entered service following overhaul, it was eventually disposed of to C.Hoyle, a dealer of Wombwell, Yorkshire at whose premises it was scrapped. (W.R.Legg)

Bow garaged RTL75, having just departed Victoria station is now traversing Grosvenor Gardens on Route 25 to Becontree Heath. The bus had re-entered service in August, having suffered the indignity of being stored since the previous November when it was made surplus to requirements with the changeover from RTL to RT operation at Barking garage. It was to continue to serve the travelling public until withdrawal in September 1968 and then again put into store to await its eventual sale for scrap in November 1969. (K.Lane)

The March sunshine casts the shadow of RTL840 on the new brickwork of the nearly completed M4 flyover at Chiswick while in service on Route 91. Garaged at Wandsworth, an RTL stronghold for many years, this bus was due for an overhaul the following month but returned to the same South London garage after being spruced up. (D.W.K.Jones)

RTL1124 had been overhauled during December 1958 but was not to re-enter service until August of the year under review. During the intervening months it gathered dust, unlicensed firstly at Hendon garage followed by four months at Finchley where it is seen heading a line of trolleybuses. It then was moved to Stockwell before entry into service at Victoria during August as one of the last batch involved with the changeover from RT to RTL operation at the garage.
(J.A.S.Hambley collection)

T.Burrows & Sons of Wombwell operated ex-D153 initially in its original condition until in July 1957 it was rebodied with a new Burlingham 62-seat body. Here at the Barnsley bus station on 7th June it carries a route blind indicating a journey from Wakefield, which is some ten miles distant in a northerly direction to Wombwell and Rawmarsh which lie south of Barnsley. Burrows & Son were acquired by the Yorkshire Traction Co.Ltd. on 22nd October 1966 bringing to an end the vehicle's operational life at Wombwell which had started in October 1953. (R.Holmes)

In the sylvan surroundings of Chislehurst Common, sprinkled with a dusting of snow, RT4542 waits on the stand at Chislehurst War Memorial with no facilities for the crew who take a rest within the lower saloon. The front adverts are in use for a campaign for more staff, reminding us that in 1959 the L.T. Recruitment Centre was at 280 Marylebone Road. (J.Gascoine collection)

Holden designed St.Albans garage opened in 1936 and was eventually demolished in 1999. It is seen here during happier times, still with the original passenger shelters in situ although the bus stops were a later addition. Potters Bar's RT941 attracts some clientele on 7th February before the start of its journey to Arnos Grove Station on Route 84, the only Central Area service to reach this Hertfordshire city in post-war years. During September the bus would receive an overhaul re-entering service at Upton Park to continue its passenger service. (A.R.Packer)

Route 7A was renumbered plain 7 with the October 14th Central Bus winter programme which included a number of non-essential alterations. Before the change, Middle Row garaged RTL1006 with nastily dented dome journeys to East Acton, Goldsmiths Arms complete with sticker in the rearmost lower saloon window announcing the impending change of service number. (F.W.Ivey)

The background to this picture is a poignant reminder of the impressive St.Albans garage that invoked so much fruitless effort by those who hoped it might have been preserved and put to good use. RF602 stops in front of the building on 7th February as it journeys to Whitwell, which was the Monday to Friday terminal of the 304 route. The section on to Hitchin was only served by three Saturday evening and four Sunday p.m. journeys. The almost indistinguishable notice placed at the top of the nearside front windscreen confirms this RF's conversion to one-person operation in September 1958. In January 1969 this was one of the vehicles transferred to the Central Area where it ran for six months on Route 210 in its green livery before being repainted red. (A.R.Packer)

An antiquated lighting column and traffic island at London Bridge Station separate two RTLs seen laying over on 21st November at this intermediate turning point on Route 40. Nearer the camera RTL67 will journey to Wanstead Station while in the background RTL623 carries the destination for a shortened journey to Wanstead Flats. Both buses are garaged at Camberwell but are here working the northern end of the route. (W.R.Legg)

New Monday to Saturday Route 169A commenced operation on 19th August in connection with the third stage of the trolleybus replacement programme. It did not directly replace a trolleybus route but provided a new 'round the corner' facility, giving a direct service from north of Ilford to Manor Park, Stratford and Bow. This was a link that had been lost ever since the outbreak of the Second World War when 25A had been curtailed at Ilford. RTL1302 from Bow garage stands in front of an RT on Route 169 behind which can be seen a relic of trolleybus operation. (R.Wellings)

RT401, the last of the initial batch bodied by Park Royal, is seen leaving the stand in London Bridge Station forecourt en-route to Golders Green Station by way of Route 13 on 10th April. First entering service in May 1948 and having received two overhauls previously, it presently carries an RT8 type body numbered 6408 in place of the original RT3 version numbered 1650. It wasn't disposed of until the fortieth year of RT operation in 1979 and having received further body changes, departed to pastures new in June of that year carrying Weymann body number 7163. (A.B.Cross)

An unusual scene of three GSs awaiting further use in Gravesend on 5th September with the lead pair of buses both showing Route 450 details. GS54 heads the line with GS46 next and furthest away from the camera GS53. The trio had initially entered service in December 1953 garaged at Northfleet as part of one of the largest concentrations of the class. GS46 in fact spent its whole career at this one garage until sold in March 1968. (R.A.Golds)

RTL1252 from Bow garage shares the parking area at the Aldgate Bus Station with Forest Gate's RT1822. Both are working the additional journeys provided between here and Victoria to strengthen the City and West End section of the 25 route. The buses went their separate ways after disposal by London Transport with the RTL being exported to Ceylon in December 1965 while the RT, still in London Transport livery, was used by a travel agent in Belgium on a publicity campaign until an encounter with a low bridge ended its career. (A.Mortimer)

This use of the route number 122 had been introduced on 9th September 1936 having lain dormant since 30th September 1934 when its previous manifestation had been absorbed into the 23 service. The Earl of Chatham, Woolwich has been the regular western terminal since inception. RT399 is seen at the eastern terminus of Bexleyheath trolleybus depot forecourt on 4th March surrounded by several of the depot's trolleybus allocation now awaiting disposal following cessation of electric operation the previous evening. 397C, a D2C class Leyland vehicle with Northern Coachbuilders body received in 1946 following its destruction two years earlier when Bexleyheath depot was bombed, stands behind still wearing its final 696 destination. Later in the month it would be scrapped by George Cohen. (A.R.Packer)

The unmistakable façade of the 'Royal Forest Hotel' at Chingford provides the background to Palmers Green garaged RT1169 resting between journeys on Route 102 on this bright May day. The destination blind has been re-wound already for a return journey to Golders Green Station, which was important at this terminus since on normal days boarding on stand was allowed. Enfield's RT2818 with running plates E37 is similarly prepared for a journey to Hammond Street on Route 205. This will run the length of Sewardstone Road from Kings Head Hill to Waltham Abbey on its way. Nowadays only a school journey on First Capital's 253 route performs this particular journey although Arriva's 505 route provides an alternative route through Bury Road and Daws Hill, which was uncharted bus territory in 1959. (R.A.Golds)

While on hire to Great Yarmouth Corporation GS68 and GS63 are viewed on the Gorleston circular service meeting at Halfway House when the route operated in both directions using the number 8. At this time Ultimate ticket machines were in use while the Corporation had made the very informative route blinds at the Caister Road garage. To highlight the huge increase in operating costs since 1959, it has been estimated that each bus cost £50 a month for the duration of the loan. When returned to London Transport, operation of the one-person routes, which the GSs had pioneered, was taken over by newly delivered Albion/Willowbrook 31 seaters. (P.D.Long)

RTL561 was one of a number of the class received by Middle Row garage in exchange for RTWs which were despatched to Walworth in September. With the demise of the RTWs, which had only been resident at X since the previous November, the garage once again reverted to housing only RTLs until the arrival of RMs in 1963. The bus is seen in use on Route 7A prior to the October renumbering with an older style five line via point blind. (J.A.S.Hambley collection)

To cater for the ever expanding district of Chaulden within the new town of Hemel Hempstead, Saturday only Route 307B had been introduced on 11th May 1957. With further new building work in progress behind, RF700, the only RF delivered ready equipped for one-man operation, waits departure from the town centre bus station to the Lower Sales terminal at Chaulden on the last day of January. (A.R.Packer)

The withdrawal of route 127 in the previous August and the subsequent replacement by other types of buses on certain lowbridge routes in the Country Area reduced the number of RLH class vehicles required for scheduled service. Due to heavy passenger loadings at certain times of the day, RF operated Route 208A was in need of extra capacity. By making certain alterations to the route it was possible for the spare RLHs to be introduced. Accordingly RLH, 1, 7, 9, 29, 49, 52, 53, 54, 56, 57, 58, 59 and 65 were relicensed and together with RLH68 transferred from Harrow Weald were allocated to Dalston garage. On 13th May the replacement route numbered 178 commenced operation. RLH1, which had been a Country Area vehicle until repainted red in November 1956, waits at Maryland Point for a journey to Clapton Pond. (R.Wellings)

Tower Bridge has obviously been closed for some reason since Camberwell's RTL736 is crossing the River Thames by way of London Bridge en-route for Camberwell Green. Morris, Austin and Vauxhall cars are represented by the following traffic, while the lack of pedestrians suggests the picture was probably taken on a Sunday when maintenance work was possibly being carried out on the famous bascule bridge which was the route's normal passage across the water. (F.W.Ivey)

Windsor garaged RT3731 is parked in St. George's Drive just short of Elizabeth Bridge which was used as the Victoria Green Line boarding point for some time in 1959 due to reconstruction work on Eccleston Bridge. It is waiting before taking up a return journey to Windsor via Slough as a relief coach on Route 704. In later years the fleet number was worn by a red liveried substitute thereby ending the Country Area connection which had initially commenced in June 1953. (W.R.Legg)

RTL1243 had initially entered service in December 1951 with others of the class at Hornchurch garage for Route 175. Having received one overhaul and experienced passenger service at no less than ten different garages in the intervening years, it was transferred to Camberwell garage in August and is seen with Q18 running plates for its involvement on Route 35. A slipboard is carried announcing 'To and From Geffrye Museum', which is situated in Kingsland Road and contains period rooms from the 16th to 20th century, together with early ironwork, woodwork and 18th century shopfronts, all housed in almshouses erected in 1715. (A.Mortimer)

RTL1057 helps out on the 406F special service between Epsom Downs and the town station while on temporary loan from Mortlake to Leatherhead garage. The bus had re-entered service from its final overhaul in August 1958 and was now a combination of the chassis of the original RTL1066 with body from RTL1025. It continued in passenger service for a few more years before being demoted to learner duties, first at Hertford and then at Hatfield garages. Withdrawn in February 1965 it subsequently made the long sea journey to Ceylon for operation by the Ceylon Transport Board. (A. Mortimer)

Ex-STL737 admirably shows its years of dereliction in the ownership of R.W.Toop, W.J.Ironside and P.W.Davis, better known as Bere Regis and District Motor Services, who had acquired it as a means of providing spare parts. First entering service as a 9STL5 it was one of the last of an order totalling 150. The type represented a turning point in the development of the London double decker bus in that diesel power had ousted petrol once and for all from the first of the batch numbered STL609. The bodywork built by the L.P.T.B. incorporated a gently curved front profile although it was still fitted with a destination box below the route blind aperture. (C.Bull collection)

Nearing the end of its existence, being sold for scrap in July of the following year, ex-D126 is seen with its fifth operator, namely the executors of Samuel Ledgard of Leeds. The date is 14th March and parked next to the premises of Eltram Textiles in Park Place near Leeds city centre in its blue and white livery, it clearly demonstrates how little the exterior bodywork has changed over the years since disposal by London Transport in May 1953. The saloon side windows, previously half drop, have been replaced at some stage with sliding vents and the front upper deck are now of the non-opening variety. The repositioned number plate slightly unbalances the frontal appearance. (A.R.Packer)

The uses that London passenger vehicles have found themselves in after sale are many and here the chassis of former STD23 is now the basis of a lorry with the capability to tow a trailer. This particular STD was not one which wandered away from Hendon garage during the Second World War as was the case with some but it did finish its London Transport service at Enfield garage. Two months after withdrawal it was sold in December 1953 to W.North of Leeds. The Magnet Joinery Co.Ltd. of Bingley, Yorkshire acquired it sometime later and here on 7th June of the year under review it is seen in rebuilt condition as a full fronted lorry. In the background a Ford Popular can be seen to the left with a pre-war car standing next to an Austin and in the far distance what appears to be a Bristol Lodekka bus. (J.A.S.Hambley collection)

RT1056 in the forecourt of St.Albans garage on 7th February is blinded ready for its next journey to Borehamwood on Route 358. Redevelopment of the former garage site during 1999 and 2000 has resulted in residential housing covering the site. This fleet numbered vehicle was allocated to Grays, St.Albans and later Reigate before it began a new life in the Central Area at Brixton from September 1965 onwards. (A.R.Packer)

Standing in the Grays garage yard on 5th September complete with route blinds set for use on Route 328, RT1088 is also fitted with GY220 running plates. A slipboard carried in the holder on the front bulkhead announces 'To & From the Orsett Show', which together with the bus parked on the left of the picture with 'EXTRA' slipboard and running plates GY241 suggest a well-patronised additional service for this event. The front adverts publicise a rival event but any potential visitors to the Radio Show at Earls Court will need to get up to London quickly if they are not to miss the last day. Perhaps the local event is a more practical destination. (R.A.Golds)

RLH25 waits in the Onslow Street Bus Station at Guildford before undertaking a short working on Route 436 to Burpham, which is 2½ miles distant. The full extent of the route was through to Staines, which is still covered by the Arriva Guildford and West Surrey route of the same number today. (A.R.Packer)

RT4005, with highly reflective paintwork having only recently re-entered service after an overhaul in February, waits use at Woolwich on Route 186. A badly wound destination blind displays a choice of Crystal Palace or Lewisham, which one hopes will be tidied up when the driver returns to his cab. In April 1964 this combination of chassis and body numbered 1542 left these shores to take up further duties around Cape Town in South Africa. (A.Mortimer)

On 30th January T790 stands opposite Berkhamsted Station in surprisingly rural surroundings while operating the Saturday working on Route 352, which ran from here to Dunstable. The bus was the last 15T13 to be operated by Tring garage, finally being withdrawn from service in June 1962. (A.R.Packer)

With what appears to be a home made route number blind RT4153 turns at Upminster Station on the short 248A route right on the periphery of London Transport Central Area operations in Essex. The route, which had been numbered 249, had been withdrawn in August 1958 but was re-introduced in April of the year under review with the number 248A. In this form it lasted a considerable number of years until withdrawn in June 1986 when the service was taken over by the 246A. (R.Wellings)

Parked in Bolton Road, Bradford former RT165 wears the livery of the Bradford City Transport undertaking and carries fleet number 407. Alterations have been made to the destination equipment of the Park Royal bodywork including the removal of the roof box. The interiors of these buses were changed considerably in appearance, having a much more 'provincial/municipal' feel about them, as can be seen on the solitary preserved example which attends rallies from time to time. (D.F.Parker)

RT1359 with running plates SP12 is traversing Blackfen Road on its way to Bexley Hospital. This was the additional Sunday service on Route 132 and the conductor has not only wound the via point blind to blank to indicate this but has also removed the route number. The canopy blind still displays 132 however, which indicates the view was taken before 4th March on which date these duties were taken over by new Route 124A. (A.Mortimer)

RM130 is seen at the North Woolwich terminus of new Route 48 introduced with the fourth stage of the trolleybus conversion programme. It replaced trolleybus route 569 together with some journeys on the 567 and 665 and provided a new direct link through the City to Waterloo. The word 'Routemaster' was carried above the fleet number on both sides of the cab for a number of years and it was not until late 1964 that new deliveries omitted the word.

(A.Mortimer)

Two RTs rest at Ramsgate Harbour coach park, a considerable distance from their normal sphere of operation in this summer Sunday view. RT1912 to the left of the picture carries a Park Royal RT8/2 type body numbered 9134, originally mounted on the chassis of RTL1564. RT4679, its closely parked companion, is fitted with an identical body numbered 8514 first carried by RT4637. Slipboards on the bulkheads identify the occasion as an outing for the Catford Garage Sports Club while different styles of 'Private' blind display are shown. (L.Mallett)

Red RT4336 was allocated to Stevenage for a month in August of the year under review. Here it loads in Stevenage bus station before leaving for the Bandley Hill terminal to which the route had been extended from Hydean Way on 15th April. (A.Mortimer)

On 30th January RLH42 pauses at Rickmansworth en-route to Watford on Route 336. This route was the first to receive RLHs when they replaced ST class buses then approaching twenty years of age in June 1950. It was not until October 1965 that the RLHs were replaced themselves by one man operated RFs. (A.R.Packer)

The through service on Route 390 to Stevenage was single deck worked but the extra journeys from Hertford terminating at the then closed Watton railway station just off the A602 were usually operated with double deck buses. Hertford garaged RT1012 waiting at Hertford Bus Station will hardly be taxed along the journey passing through the villages of Waterford and Stapleford following the course of the River Beane. (R.Wellings)

RF629 had received an overhaul in the previous December and now with body number 8873, first carried by fleet number RF696, it is seen at Amersham prior to commencing a Route 359 journey through to Aylesbury. The date is 3rd January and with direction indicators temporarily tucked out of use, 'Pay as you Enter' sticker in place and painted wheel trim, it represents the latest standard exterior appearance of these Country Area buses in 1959. (A.R.Packer)

Red liveried RT4233 was transferred to Stevenage garage in August, being one of four previously in store at Stockwell which re-entered service as replacements in the Country Area enabling suitable green RTs to be released around the system ultimately to enhance Route 726. It is seen at the town's bus station during the short period of loan which ended in October when again it was put into store, this time at Loughton. As it waits to depart on Route 801 to Hitchin, St. Mary's Square the new bus garage can be seen in the background, although the buildings on the right, which in due course will house the Magistrate's Court and a ten pin bowling alley among other attractions, have yet to be built. (A.Mortimer)

This very busy scene populated largely by women shoppers waiting for their particular bus at Hemel Hempstead bus station was photographed on a cold and damp 30th January. RT604 in service on Route 330 still needs its destination blind resetting before departure but at least some passengers are boarding without that information. The choice of via point blind is unfortunate since it is that intended for short workings between St.Albans and Hatfield. After over thirty years service RT604 was disposed of to the Wombwell Diesels Company, being quickly rescued to join the preservation movement and is now a regular rally attendee. (A.R.Packer)

This route 163 originated as the replacement for tram service 40 on 6th July 1952. Seven years later in brilliant sunshine and warm weather, New Cross based RT3305 stops beside the familiar Woolwich Building Society headquarters in General Gordon Place while working a short journey to Camberwell Green. The first via point 'Kennington' will not be served on this journey. (A.Mortimer)

RF638 had received an overhaul in December of the previous year to re-enter service complete with newly fitted trafficators at Leatherhead garage. It departs the garage to take up duties on Route 462 on a local journey to Fetcham rather than the full route through to Staines. (A.Mortimer)

Tottenham's RTW26 waits to do a turn on the Football Express service between Spurs Ground and Manor House with a sister vehicle parked behind. The white on blue blinds tell you that the single fare is 1/- and the service was put on to ease the pressure on the local trolleybus routes and speed the football fans to and from the Piccadilly Line tube. It would be another nine years before a closer tube station was available at Seven Sisters or Tottenham Hale. (A.Mortimer)

RTL163 had ceased its revenue earning years of operation while garaged at Riverside in August 1958 and was delicensed and stored until further use as staff transport once again got its wheels turning. In its new role, with the customary garage slipboard carried on the front bulkhead, it is seen heading along Fulham Palace Road sometime in September of the year under review. The bus, a combination of the chassis which had entered service as RTL153 and the body number 5049, originally fitted to RT2170, was disposed of in October 1970 for scrap. (A.Mortimer)

Craven bodied ex-RT1514 is seen at Peterborough in the ownership of Longland's of Crowland whose bus it has been since August 1956. It will shortly be re-sold to Mulley's Motorways of Ixworth. Its pedigree remains unmistakable although the roof route number box has been removed together with offside route number holder and running plate bracketry. A Bristol K chassis with ECW bodywork operated by Eastern Counties stands in the background with a totally different approach to saloon ventilation. (A.Mortimer)

Former T701 is seen in October of the year under review working in Uganda for the Eastern Province Bus Company (1954) Ltd. as their fleet number 23. The registration letters UE indicate the district of Jinga, which is a major marketing centre on the shores of Lake Victoria. The destination blind appears to call the town 'Inja' but it may be that the initial J is hidden. Apart from the added luggage pen on the roof and the smart front bumper, the coach is still very much in London Transport condition some five years after it was disposed of to W.North, the Leeds dealer. (J.A.S.Hambley collection)

Long standing daily route 148 operated between Leytonstone and Dagenham but from the third Sunday in March 1955 half the Sunday service was diverted between Redbridge and Ilford via The Drive resulting in new Route 148A. In practice this restored a service which had been withdrawn when Route 147 was reduced to weekday operation only in the winter programme introduced the previous October. Towards the end of the year under review Seven Kings garaged RT1945 works the Sunday route with an appropriate slipboard reading 'via THE DRIVE' for the convenience of the unwary traveller who misses the significance of the 'A' suffix. (A.Mortimer)

With stage 3 of the trolleybus conversion, which took place on 19th August, Route 86A would be renumbered plain 86, resurrecting the use of the parent number which had disappeared in the upheavals of the previous year. Soon to depart from the Wangey Road stand at Chadwell Heath prior to August, RT2293 will be running in to Romford, North Street garage at the end of its next journey. Television has not yet conquered everything and the bus advertises the forthcoming 'Radio Show' at Earls Court. (A.Mortimer)

In compiling this volume I have realised that a picture of GS71 appears on page 88 of the 1954 book of this series showing it in service from Epping garage, presumably on short-term loan. Delivered to the Executive in December 1953 contemporary records show it to have resided throughout its career at Garston garage until sold in March 1965. Having just arrived at the Rickmansworth Station terminus on 30th January, the last or only passenger is about to emerge from the saloon doorway with his trusted suitcase which appears to be of dimensions unsuited to GS travel. (A.R.Packer)

Sunday Route 95A varied from the weekday 95 which ran to Cannon Street by diverting at Borough to run to London Bridge Station and then, during the midday period, continuing to Blackwall Tunnel thereby serving the popular Sunday markets of the East End. On a decidedly dreary and damp 27th December RT1955 stands empty at London Bridge presumably either in early morning or mid-afternoon. Back in service from its September overhaul, Saunders bodywork of RT3/3 type number 7368 is now carried by the fleet number which originally used a Park Royal body of RT8 classification. (W.R.Legg)

West Ham was the minor partner in the 11th November trolleybus conversion which was the first to use the Routemaster buses designed for the purpose. They shared an involvement at this stage with Poplar on Routes 5 and 238. RM57 heads for Chittys Lane at Becontree displaying a very untidy blind, two places on which (Commercial Road and Poplar) were not served by the 238. (A.R.Packer)

RTL3 had its bodywork rebuilt to offside platform and staircase configuration as a demonstrator for potential overseas buyers. Here it is parked inside Gillingham Street, Victoria garage sometime in June of the year under review. The rebuild to the body, which was number 2077 originally mounted on RT798, was carried out in October 1958. The converted vehicle was eventually disposed of in April 1964 to an auto-rental organisation in Switzerland having proved to be something of a commercial failure. (D.W.K.Jones)

From left to right, tree lopper 970J, RT64 and GS51 attract dust while parked out of use within Northfleet garage on 30th June. The GS vacated its parking area first when in August it was transferred to Chelsham to re-enter passenger use. The service vehicle followed next in October returning to manicure the trees in the immediate locality but it was not until December 1960 that the RT, which appears to have severely damaged its nose, vacated the garage and was despatched to Bird's Commercial Motors of Stratford-upon-Avon. (R.B.Partridge)

From the beginning of bus operation in 1926, Bradford City Transport had been an enthusiastic operator of the AEC marque and it was therefore no great surprise when they purchased twenty-five ex-RTs in 1958. It was not the first time an RT had been on the streets of the city, RT19 having visited in September 1940 while in its capacity as a demonstrator. Here former RT414, with front and side destination indicators rebuilt to the Corporation's general layout, climbs Thornton Road nearing the outer terminal of Route 69. Withdrawal of the type was spread between 1963 and 1969 with fleet number 417 being disposed of to Autospares of Bingley for scrap in May 1969. (D.F.Parker)

Immediately upon its return to service after receiving an overhaul in June of the year under review, RTL975 was put to use on the Southfields Station and Wimbledon Tennis Ground special service. Interestingly brackets are in place for the eventual fitting of the trafficators and the garage code WD has been painted between the brackets which normally held the stencil. Research has established that painted garage codes had started to appear on buses operating from certain Central Area garages during 1959 prior to their universal adoption in 1960. The lettering used here is of a much smaller size than the later standard. (J.A.S.Hambley collection)

The fitting of direction indicators to the passenger fleet is now well under way as can be seen by the many instances in this volume of partially fitted equipment or complete units. RT873 is seen on 21st November at London Bridge Station a few days after its return to passenger service from overhaul where the opportunity has been taken to fit the primary equipment for the eventual 'ears'. Colney Hatch Lane, Hampden Road has been selected as the destination for what will be a run into the garage. By 1959 this should only have been used for buses working into the garage from the north. The alternative 'Muswell Hill, Hampden Road', which was more meaningful at this distance, was provided for buses working through Muswell Hill Broadway on their way in. (W.R.Legg)

In February of the year under review a rail replacement service operated on the Hertford North line of British Rail. Photographic evidence shows that buses from at least three garages, Palmers Green, Potters Bar and Tottenham were used. In the upper picture RT4434 which was only allocated to Potters Bar for the month, waits in the forecourt of Enfield Chase Station while below Tottenham's RTL964 backs into the station entrance at Cuffley while would-be rail passengers wait to find which direction it will be serving. (A.Mortimer)

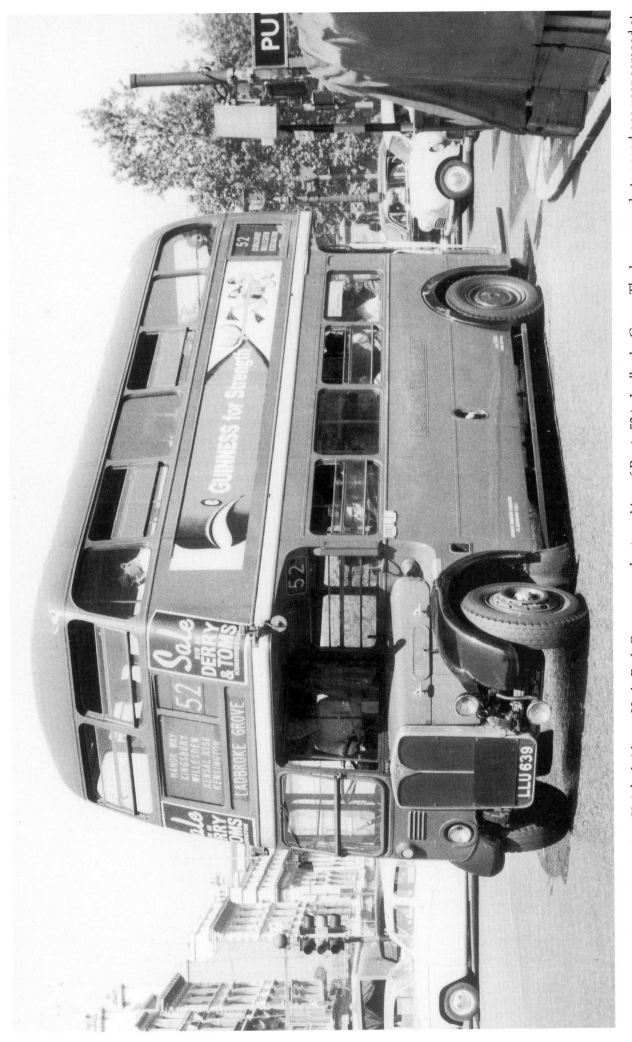

Victoria garaged RT3280 turns into Knightsbridge at Hyde Park Corner on a short working of Route 52 to Ladbroke Grove. The bus was only to spend one year garaged at Gillingham Street before transfer to Barking. After use at a number of further garages it was disposed of in August 1973. (J.G.S.Smith collection)

Just twelve months away from being scrapped, 1937 built former STL1739 shows signs of age with its only post London operator, T.Canham (Services) Ltd. of Whittlesey. On 30th May it is seen resting before moving to the pick up point within the bus station at Peterborough and departure on another eight mile journey to the town of Whittlesey, traversing the flat roads so prominent in this part of England. A livery of practically all-over cream with just a narrow blue band above the lower window line together with operator's name and service details sufficed for its 6½ year prolonged existence in East Anglia. (A.R.Packer)

RT4773, while not the highest numbered, was the very last member of the class to enter passenger service in August of the year under review. It had a few days use at Northfleet garage before transfer in the same month to Staines, where it resided through to March of the following year. Originally delivered to London Transport in July 1954 it had lain idle and unwanted for most of the intervening period at Loughton garage until moved to Grays during May 1959 for preparation for public use. Here at an Autumn Ascot race meeting, in company with other members of the class, it still awaits its first advertising material to disfigure its pristine condition. (A.D.Packer)

RM2 had been repainted from Country Area livery to Central Area red in August 1957 and was allocated to Turnham Green garage. From then up to 1st November 1959, when it ended its active passenger carrying career, it was used when serviceable on Route 91 (weekdays) and Route 27 (Sundays). Seen here on Highgate Hill at the Archway on 21st March with running plates V117 it waits departure time for Teddington Station on the 27. By now it is fitted with air suspension in lieu of coil springs at the rear and the gearbox has been changed from hydraulic to electro-pneumatic. (A.R.Packer)

After a few more steps the driver of Turnham Green's RT465 will presumably be able to stand upright, perhaps illustrating the arduousness of driving this type of bus. The terminus at Argyle Road, Ealing looks a little bleak in this wintry view. The offer by Zetter's Pools of over £7,000 for a farthing shows that such currency was still meaningful in 1959. In addition the juxtaposition of the front advertisements is interesting - was it Ben Truman's hops which were on the bus? (A.Mortimer)

The isolated trolleybus system in the Bexleyheath area was converted to motor bus operation on 4th March of the year under review. New bus route 96, operated with thirty-six Bexleyheath garaged RTs (reducing to thirty-one of Saturday and twenty on Sunday) replaced the 696 Woolwich to Dartford route. RT4528 depicted here had been transferred to the garage as one of the initial allocation. A Green Line RF on Route 702 is about to join the bus beneath the now unused bowstring support arms fitted to the traction poles in the one-way road system at Bexleyheath Market Place. (F.W.Ivey)

It is known that London Transport exported at least eighty-three of the two hundred and sixty six original Green Line 10T10 coaches after disposal. Of this number a minimum of twenty-five saw further service in Yugoslavia and this example is seen at Split in August. Its former LT fleet number is presently unknown although it carries Croatian registration H5940 together with fleet number 31 which is midway along the saloon bodywork. These exports took place during the years 1953 to 1955 and it is interesting to see the bus is basically complete save for the nearside engine cover and lifeguard. Green Line route board brackets, route number and running plate holders are still in situ with the saloon door permanently fixed shut now that an offside doorway as been added. (D.W.K.Jones)

It was at the rear that the eight feet wide RTWs were most distinguishable from other members of the RT family. The buffers for the emergency window, positioned either side of the indicators, meant the rear side adverts had to be placed on the corner pillars. Originally a Leyland style rainwater gutter with an upward nearside and downward offside curve was fitted above the emergency window. Most however were replaced, as in this example, by the more standard London Transport wrap-round style. Traversing Gascoigne Road, Upton Park's RTW54 now nears the terminal of Route 100 at the Broadway in this view taken on 8th August. This short works service from the huge Beckton gasworks originated in the somewhat unique Barking Council tram route which crossed Barking Creek on a bascule bridge and was replaced by motor buses as early as 1929. (J.H.Price)

Samuel Ledgard of Ilkley, West Yorkshire acquired two batches of former D class buses via the dealer W.North of Leeds before a further example joined the fleet which had previously been owned by two other operators. Parked within the Otley bus station on 12th September ex-D236 nearest the camera is kept company by ex-D277 and a contemporary Roe bodied machine delivered new to the company. Both Park Royal bodied vehicles have been re-panelled in the area above the rear platform, effectively removing the blind box while the front three-piece boxes have given way to a single horizontal strip. Both vehicles attained a life span of some fifteen years in passenger use before they were finally scrapped. (J.C.Gillham)

GS40 stands at Uxbridge Station on 17th January working Route 459 to Richings Park Estate, a route that had been previously operated by a crewed RF. Subsequent to the resumption of normal working after the 1958 strike a number of GS operated routes were withdrawn or converted to one-man RF operation in October. It was therefore pleasant to witness this new addition to the ranks of GS routes. Unfortunately this situation was short lived as on 4th March of the year under review a one-man operated RF took over responsibility for the route and once again Windsor's sole use for the class was their route 445. (A.R.Packer)

These two ex-G class buses had originally entered service at Upton Park garage in consecutive months with former G332 seen to the left of the picture being the first in December 1945. In 1954 it was acquired by W.Alexander & Sons of Falkirk via the dealer, W.North but was never operated. It then passed via Locke, a dealer of Edinburgh, to a showman. Ex-G340 was also acquired by W.Alexander & Sons but did enter service in May 1953 and then found further use with a showman in 1955. By 1959 the two buses had met up and they are seen as fairground tenders at a gathering near Oban, Ayrshire on 25th August. They are in the ownership of Mr.J.Cordona, whose family was still active as fairground operators on the west coast of Scotland as recently as 1994. (A.J.Malsher)

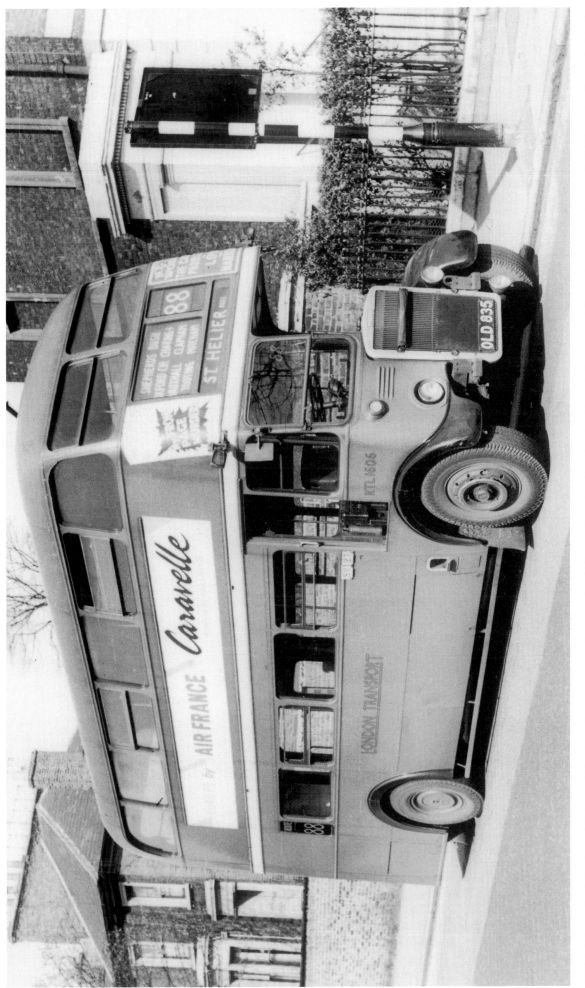

RTL1606, parked in the vicinity of Stockwell garage, carries service information for the Route 88 rush hour and Saturday extension to St.Helier, the Rose. Initially entering service in February 1958, this bus was to receive its one and only overhaul in September 1961 to be disposed of in October 1965, albeit with a different combination of chassis and body to that now shown. (A.Mortimer)

Dusk begins to fall as RM84 waits departure from the Becontree Heath bus station on 14th November. Route 23 had been strengthened with changes associated with the fourth stage of the trolleybus replacement programme, which took place on the night of 10th/11th November. A Poplar garage allocation was introduced to the route with nine RM required Monday to Friday and twenty on Saturday. The intermediate route blind displayed is that for the 238 route but it would be appropriate for short workings at the eastern end of the 23. (A.R.Packer)

The long standing terminal for Route 471 at Orpington Station finds GS23, with running plates DG11, attracting patronage in this view taken on 10th January before departure on the circular route serving such delightful sounding places as Cudham, Knockholt and Pratts Bottom. Nowadays this route is still served but by Arriva - Kent Thameside under the number R5. The GS had initially entered service at Hertford garage in November 1953, receiving an overhaul in October 1956 then re-entering service at Dunton Green garage. Its uninterrupted passenger service, apart from a further overhaul in October 1960, was completed at this garage with withdrawal taking place in September 1964 and disposal the following month. (A.R.Packer)

RM20 was first used as a training vehicle garaged at Upton Park and later Clay Hall before entry into public service took place in November, operating out of West Ham. In company with a further example of the class it rests under cover minus its nearside direction indicator.

(Lens of Sutton)

Seen parked on the St.Helier Esplanade, Jersey are two superbly presented ex-RTLs which were prepared by London Transport prior to despatch in the green and cream livery of Jersey Motor Traction with London Transport style route blinds. J8629 is ex-RTL1348 and J8683 ex-RTL1515, both having arrived on the island in the early spring of the year under review as part of a batch of eight to be acquired. Two more batches of three were obtained in future years. The RTLs were used on heavily trafficked routes. After many years service both these buses returned to the mainland to find entirely different uses which are documented in the book 'RTL and RTW classes after London Transport' parallel to this series of books. (M.Dryhurst)

RT289 seen with running plates TB3 and in its final combination of chassis and body numbered 1529, waits at the Bromley North terminal stand before taking up a further journey on Route 119 to Croydon, Barclay Road. The fleet number dates from January 1948 when the original bus entered service at Middle Row garage along with forty-seven others to oust the ST and STL class vehicles from the 15 and 28 routes. It arrived at Bromley garage after receiving its last overhaul in October 1958, ending its passenger career in London during February 1963 when it entered storage prior to disposal during the first month of the following year. (R.Wellings)

RT264 is caught by the camera at Chingford Mount in use on Route 38 on a short working to Rosebery Avenue. C.Hoyle, one of the dealers congregated in the Wombwell area of Yorkshire, scrapped the bus soon after its disposal by London Transport in November 1963. (J.Gascoine collection)

The 322B was a Saturday afternoon only route introduced on 13th June of the year under review and, as the blind of RF645 shows, ran between Kings Langley, The Nap and Watford Junction. It worked from The Nap in Kings Langley centre via the High Street, Church Lane and Water Lane to join the main 322 in Station Road whose route it then followed to Watford Junction. The route only lasted until 21st May 1960. (A.Mortimer)

The Ascot race meeting on Saturday 20th June has resulted in this array of different vehicles pressed into service for the benefit of the racegoers. Centrepiece Green Line liveried RT3226 usually plies the roads of East London, being garaged at London Road, Romford. RT4744 standing beside in Country Area colour scheme has passed its fifth birthday although it has only witnessed eighteen months passenger use, firstly garaged at Watford High Street and later Garston. The one vehicle which can be identified in the far background is RF93, one of Guildford garage's allocation of coaches normally to be found on Route 715. (A.R.Packer)

Bennetts Gate via Leys Road is the ultimate destination of RT606 in use on cross-town route 314A at Hemel Hempstead bus station in January. Since its initial entry into service during September 1948, it has never wandered further afield from Two Waters garage and the Hemel Hempstead area although after its next overhaul during January 1960 it finally broke its ties, re-entering service at Grays. The fleet number had been within the first batch of fifty-five delivered to the Country Area, which were the last of the first Weymann bodybuilding order. (A.R.Packer)

393W is one of the 6½ ton stores lorries rebuilt from Green Line coaches. This example was completed in June 1939, previously being T282. It survived until August 1960 when it was disposed of to Vehicle & Plant Supply of Southall, Middlesex. It is seen on 3rd June at Epsom Racecourse on Derby day, allocated to the Central Distribution Services at Chiswick and seems to be carrying a precarious load of scaffolding and screens for what purpose is unclear. (J.C.Gillham)

Route 419 provided a town service in Epsom running from Brettgrave to Langley Vale. This route was the first chosen for experimental one-man operation with RFs commencing in March 1954. Here in the town centre on 15th February RF674 with LH52 running plates unloads its passengers. (A.R.Packer)

The centrepiece of this view taken in the Dartford garage yard on 14th February is RT4035 which carries route details for the 423B with destination set for Watchgate, Ladywood Road. This was the point to which the route had been extended on 14th May 1958. RT4179 parked closely alongside shows partial details for Route 401 presumably having run in off a short working. Both buses would ultimately receive Central Area colours - RT4035 in April of the year under review and RT4179 in March 1969. (A.R.Packer)

Parked beneath the trolleybus wiring for short journeys on Routes 645 and 660 in the lay-by just off Finchley Road, Golders Green, Enfield garaged RT722 waits departure to Chingford Hatch on the Sunday only Route 102A. Upon a visit to Aldenham in November for overhaul RT3 type body number 1994 of Park Royal manufacture was given this fleet number and disposal came in February 1965. (A.R.Packer)

In this July view RT1700 arrives in Guildford on the local Route 408A from Merrow, Bushey Hill. Originally entering service in April 1950 as a Central Area bus, the fleet number re-appeared from a September 1957 overhaul in green livery for Country Area service. On 1st January 1970 it passed to London Country Bus Services Ltd. and continued in service until January 1975. After passing through the hands of a dealer it joined the preservation movement where it continues to be a regular visitor at many gatherings. (R.Stanmore)

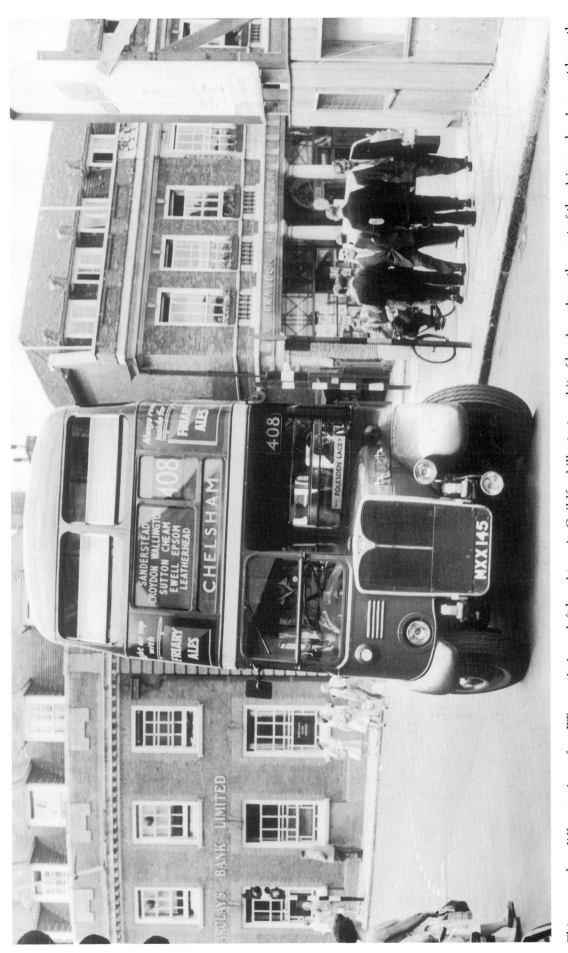

This somewhat different view of an RT negotiating a left hand turn in Guildford illustrates a bit of hard work on the part of the driver who does not have the benefit of power assisted steering. Leatherhead garaged RT3630 is on service in this July view on the long haul Route 408 from Guildford to Chelsham which has been so decimated in recent years that only the section between Epsom and Sutton remains at the time of writing. Polesden Lacey gets a mention on the slipboard as a visitor attraction preceded in small letters by the word 'NEAR'. Near in this case means just under a mile and a quarter walk! (R.Stanmore)

Football Specials were still in evidence during the year and several examples parked at Wembley Stadium in April wait the return of fans once the final whistle has been blown. RT3980 had re-entered service at Palmers Green garage after its February overhaul but was to be transferred to Uxbridge during November. Long time Potters Bar resident RT2730 alongside would also be transferred, in this case to Leyton, during June. (A.R.Packer)

The date is 27th September and RT2765 of Norbiton garage finds itself in use on a 'Railway Emergency Service' in the company of RT3371 parked closely behind. Shadows of what appears to be trolleybus overhead wiring fall diagonally on the subject bus but at the moment the location has yet to be confirmed. A British Railways parcel delivery van with Greater London registration plates adds interest to the picture. (J.H.Aston)

At Edgware station on 27th March RT2483 with RT695 beyond wait departure to Rayners Lane L.T. Station as HD8 and HD7 respectively. The two Harrow Weald buses depict the two frontal styles of the RT class in passenger use through to 1971, when the last roof box variety was withdrawn. (R.A.Golds)

Sometime during its short spell garaged at Hackney, RM47 exits Shaftesbury Avenue as it travels to Putney Common on Route 22. The lack of private cars is noticeable with just two buses and three taxis in the scene. The introduction of a three line via point blind was intended to counter criticism of the somewhat illegible four line examples used on the prototype RMs. (W.R.Legg)

The 484 group of routes in Slough had many variations. On 14th April Windsor's RT1045 lays over before a journey to Farnham Road, The George. With changes to this group of routes made on 8th July the George would be the furthest point west reached by these services. (A.R.Packer)

On 28th March the unique (in 1959) coach version of the RM class is seen at Notting Hill Gate opposite Church Street with the shadow of a well-laden lamppost etched upon its side. Having been evaluated on a number of Green Line routes in the preceding eighteen months it was the turn of the busy 715 route on 24th January to play host to CRL4 for a five-month sojourn. The coach was officially garaged at Hertford but on occasions, such as depicted here, it carried Guildford running plates as was customary when a coach finished its day at the wrong end of a long haul route. (J.C.Gillham)

The only London Transport route to use the Guildford, Farnham Road bus station was the 425 and RF584 is seen soon to depart for Dorking North Station sometime in February. For much of the route roads were used which ran beneath the escarpment of the North Downs passing through some delightful countryside and picturesque villages such as Abinger Hammer. (A.R.Packer)

Since it was so unique I have included two views of the Christmas Day RT working by Carshalton on the 630 trolleybus route between Mitcham and West Croydon. Here at Mitcham, Carshalton's RT1844 waits to pick up any would-be through passengers from Hammersmith's F/1 class trolleybus 752 which is about to turn back towards Harlesden, College Park. The latter terminus was the one which for many years on trams and trolleybuses was referred to as 'NR. WILLESDEN JUNCTION'. (A.B.Cross)

Red liveried buses used in passenger service within the green bus sphere of operations were always worthy candidates for photography. RTL1498 had previously only operated from Chalk Farm garage followed by a period out of use and storage before its reappearance at Northfleet during July of the year under review. It is seen in service on Route 487 running to Gypsy Corner having just passed the Maidstone & District offices and garage in New Road, Gravesend. The bus carries front advertising for the Radio Show held at Earls Court between August 26th and September 5th, which latter date coincidentally is when the picture was taken. (R.A.Golds)

Originally fitted with Weymann 56-seat bodywork, G402 entered service in November 1945 as part of the last large influx of Guy Arab IIs to be allocated to Barking garage. It was withdrawn from its last operational garage at Enfield in February 1952, having in the intervening years also seen service at Upton Park. Edinburgh Corporation purchased sixty of the class and had them rebodied with Duple Midland (Nudd) or Duple Hendon bodies in the traditional city colour scheme of maroon and white and the bus is seen in the city centre on 23rd July awaiting further use on service 35. (A.R.Packer)

RT65 is about to overtake an early Express Dairy battery operated milk delivery float, which conveniently displays the actual location of this picture. The bus, demoted to learner duties in 1955, had originally entered passenger service in April 1941 garaged at Putney Bridge. The 696 trolleybus in the distance is 97C, originally built as a short wheelbased B2 class vehicle but which was rebuilt by Northern Coachbuilders and given a lengthened chassis following wartime damage and reclassified D2C. (A.B.Cross)

APPENDIX I

London Transport Central and Country Area Bus Garages

A	Sutton	LH*	Leatherhead
AB	Twickenham	LS*	Luton
AC	Willesden	M	Mortlake
AD	Palmers Green	MA*	Amersham
AE	Hendon	MH	Muswell Hill
AF	Chelverton Road, Putney	N	Norwood
AK	Streatham	NB	Norbiton
AL	Merton	NF*	Northfleet
AM	Plumstead	NS	North Street, Romford
AP	Seven Kings	NX	New Cross
AR	Tottenham	ON	Alperton
AV	Hounslow	PB	Potters Bar
AW	Abbey Wood	PM	Peckham
B	Battersea	Q	Camberwell
BK	Barking	R	Riverside
BN	Brixton	RD	Hornchurch
C	Athol Street, Poplar	RE*	London Road, Romford
CF	Chalk Farm	RG*	Reigate
CL	Clay Hall	RL	Rye Lane
CM*	Chelsham	S	Shepherds Bush
CS	Chiswick (non-operational)	SA*	St.Albans
CY*	Crawley	SJ*	Swanley Junction
D	Dalston	SP	Sidcup
DG*	Dunton Green	ST*	Staines
DS*	Dorking	SV*	Stevenage
DT*	Dartford	SW	Stockwell
E	Enfield	T	Leyton
ED	Elmers End	TB	Bromley
EG*	East Grinstead	TC	Croydon
EP*	Epping	TG*	Tring
EW	Edgware	TH	Thornton Heath
G	Forest Gate	TL	Catford
GD*	Godstone	TW*	Tunbridge Wells
GF*	Guildford	U	Upton Park
GM	Gillingham Street, Victoria	UX	Uxbridge
GR*	Garston	V	Turnham Green
GY*	Grays	W	Cricklewood
H	Hackney	WA*	Watford High Street
HD	Harrow Weald	WD	Wandsworth
HE*	High Wycombe	WG	West Green
HF*	Hatfield	WL	Walworth
HG*	Hertford	WR*	Windsor
HH*	Two Waters	WY*	Addlestone
HN*	Hitchin	X	Middle Row
HW	Southall	-	Aldenham (non-operational)
J	Holloway		
K	Kingston		
L	Loughton		

* indicates a Country Area garage.

The foregoing list represents garages operational at 1st January 1959. The trolleybus replacement programme commenced during the year continuing through to 1962 and resulted in a large number of changes to the premises housing the bus and coach fleet. It was in essence a repeat of the exercise undertaken when the trams were converted to buses a decade earlier.

The changes during the year under review, which included some developments in the Country Area were as follows:

Trolleybus Depots becoming Bus Garages:

BW   Bow on 19th August.
BX   Bexleyheath on 4th March.
CN   Carshalton on 4th March.
CT   Clapton on 15th April.
PR   Poplar on 11th November.
WH   West Ham on 11th November (still continued to operate trolleybuses as well).

New Bus Garages Opened:

HF   Hatfield on 18th February (replaced former HF on opposite side of the road).
SV   Stevenage on 29th April (replaced former SV in Fishers Green Road).

Bus Garages Closed:

CL   Clay Hall after 10th November (operations mainly transferred to BW).
HN   Hitchin after 28th April (operations mainly transferred to SV).
WA   Watford High Street after 14th April (operations transferred to GR).

Trolleybus Depots not converted to bus garages and closed:

ID   Ilford after 18th August.
LB   Lea Bridge after 14th April.

APPENDIX II

Again, a special thank you is extended to the following correspondents for their interest shown in updating or correcting information given in earlier titles in this series and in some cases answering queries arising in preparation of the present volume. They include Laurie Akehurst, Terence Atkins, Eric Baker, Alan Bond, Ken Browning, Gerald Druce, Michael Dryhurst, Barry Maynard-Smith, Tony R. Packer, John Reynolds, Les Stitson, Michael Wickham, Bob Williamson, Alan Wood and P.J.Woodage.

GENERAL

I have been reminded of the fact that London Transport had parliamentary legislation which permitted it to change the identity of its buses and coaches. This appears to have been put into operation around 1951. Chassis Unit (CU) brass identification plates were fixed to the chassis frame, not in sequence with the bonnet number but generally as vehicles passed through works for overhaul after this date. This enabled the individual chassis to keep its intrinsic identity in the same way as bodies which had their allocated London Transport body number from new. Registration and bonnet number details would allow a vehicle leaving the overhaul works to assume the identity of one entering simultaneously thus eliminating wholesale delicensing and re-licensing of vehicles off the road. Books published in this series, as indeed do many others, have given more emphasis to the bodies and the fleet numbers they carried, which after all is the main part of the bus visible to the observer. It must be remembered however that quite often the chassis is also not the one that carried the particular fleet number when it initially entered service. With the Routemasters of course there was no chassis as such but front and rear sub-frames which were highly interchangeable. In general the larger the class the more interchanges would have occurred but there will always be exceptions. For example the 15T13s and RLHs were never subjected to this treatment and there were certain individual vehicles where efforts were made to retain the body/chassis combination, as in some of those buses which had participated in overseas tours.

1951 BOOK

Page 47   It has been pointed out that despite being 'dressed' for Route 109 the bus carries a via point blind for Route 190.

1957 BOOK

Page 16   In the lower picture ex-STL1959 had seen service with Hants & Sussex, not Hants & Dorset as stated.

Page 33   The location of the bottom picture is the Westbourne Drive stand at Forest Hill rather than Perry Vale as quoted.

Page 151   In the caption to the top picture Billinghurst should read Billingshurst.

1958 BOOK

Page 7   RT2468 is in Ingrave Road at Brentwood.

Page 11   In the Introduction it has been pointed out that Routes 25A, 33, 39A, 44A, 96, 104, 123 and 139A also disappeared within the year, while although 189 was withdrawn its number was appropriated by 189A before the year end. Similarly 86A as a number disappeared taking over the withdrawn 86.

Page 19   The car immediately behind the RF in the lower picture is not a MkII Standard Vanguard but a Singer SM1500.

Page 37   A Standard 10 car with December 1954 registration moves away from the bus in the right half of the lower picture.

Page 48   RLH71 has just passed a Rover saloon car parked at the kerbside in the lower picture.

Page 58   In the lower picture the date of withdrawal for Route 73A should read 3rd March 1959, not 1958.

Page 68   A parked VW Microbus stands immediately outside Hendon Central Station in the lower picture.

Page 92   The lower picture of RT4584 is taken in York Road, Ilford not Claybury Broadway as stated.

Page 104   Route 48 was introduced on 6th January 1952.

Page 111   RTL1630 entered service in March not April as stated in the first sentence of the caption. The month of the anti-apartheid rally mentioned is correct.

Page 127   The vehicle depicted in the lower picture is a forward control Dennis Falcon with Burlingham bodywork based on the famous 'Seagull' design.

Page 142   The lower picture of ST140 is taken at Walton-on-Thames.

1961 BOOK

Page 15   In the lower picture of ex-RT231 mention should also be made that although retaining its original body the chassis on which it is now mounted is that which originally entered service as RT352.

Page 31   Ex-RT221 in the lower picture and again in the upper picture on page 145 retains its original chassis/body combination.

Page 44   RT429 in the lower picture is a combination of the original chassis of RT4130 while the body was first carried by RT274.

VEHICLE INDEX

Class	Number	Page	Class	Number	Page	Class	Number	Page	Class	Number	Page
CRL	4	152	RF	636	68	RM	110	14	RT	833	98
D	13	33	RF	638	126	RM	130	121	RT	873	133
D	101	99	RF	645	145	RT	64	132	RT	875	58
D	124	86	RF	659	42	RT	65	155	RT	911	24
D	126	116	RF	674	147	RT	83	60	RT	913	61
D	153	104	RF	675	101	RT	90	71	RT	941	106
D	179	82	RF	685	92	RT	94	67	RT	960	31
D	236	139	RF	687	46	RT	134	60	RT	984	24
D	277	139	RF	695	91	RT	159	93	RT	1001	68
G	?	41	RF	700	112	RT	165	120	RT	1012	123
G	150	95	RFW	10	102	RT	204	101	RT	1014	52
G	205	84	RFW	15	39	RT	229	92	RT	1016	43
G	293	94	RFW	15	102	RT	244	20	RT	1018	69
G	332	140	RLH	1	112	RT	247	32	RT	1023	25
G	340	140	RLH	25	118	RT	264	144	RT	1045	152
G	402	154	RLH	42	123	RT	289	144	RT	1046	14
GS	18	38	RLH	43	83	RT	297	81	RT	1056	117
GS	23	142	RLH	44	40	RT	349	29	RT	1088	117
GS	33	19	RLH	74	73	RT	380	23	RT	1152	93
GS	40	140	RM	2	67	RT	399	110	RT	1169	110
GS	46	109	RM	2	137	RT	401	108	RT	1190	22
GS	48	22	RM	5	46	RT	414	132	RT	1195	78
GS	51	132	RM	20	143	RT	465	137	RT	1212	81
GS	53	109	RM	28	95	RT	469	53	RT	1238	59
GS	54	109	RM	32	17	RT	472	48	RT	1333	58
GS	63	111	RM	35	88	RT	479	54	RT	1359	120
GS	68	111	RM	37	36	RT	494	44	RT	1380	18
GS	71	130	RM	47	151	RT	520	21	RT	1396	34
RF	93	145	RM	49	32	RT	543	7	RT	1490	77
RF	132	38	RM	49	97	RT	582	27	RT	1514	94
RF	183	20	RM	57	131	RT	602	37	RT	1514	127
RF	216	65	RM	66	96	RT	604	125	RT	1531	80
RF	249	20	RM	66	16	RT	606	146	RT	1541	99
RF	576	13	RM	70	44	RT	614	48	RT	1590	50
RF	578	30	RM	71	74	RT	621	77	RT	1700	148
RF	584	153	RM	72	81	RT	659	100	RT	1822	109
RF	602	107	RM	82	12	RT	695	151	RT	1844	153
RF	610	18	RM	84	142	RT	722	148	RT	1910	102
RF	629	124	RM	102	26	RT	782	47	RT	1912	122

Class	Number	Page	Class	Number	Page	Class	Number	Page	Class	Number	Page
RT	1945	128	RT	3685	60	RTL	364	59	RTW	78	61
RT	1955	130	RT	3727	31	RTL	392	70	RTW	121	36
RT	2029	56	RT	3731	114	RTL	405	41	RTW	339	40
RT	2127	31	RT	3859	80	RTL	493	58	STD	23	116
RT	2175	84	RT	3886	66	RTL	561	111	STD	78	88
RT	2252	39	RT	3922	15	RTL	623	107	STL	737	115
RT	2293	129	RT	3980	150	RTL	688	72	STL	896	62
RT	2405	28	RT	4005	118	RTL	736	113	STL	1729	34
RT	2408	87	RT	4011	16	RTL	840	103	STL	1739	64
RT	2483	151	RT	4035	147	RTL	895	26	STL	1739	136
RT	2595	96	RT	4049	22	RTL	897	85	STL	1836	35
RT	2602	75	RT	4065	71	RTL	901	55	STL	2377	43
RT	2672	29	RT	4120	51	RTL	964	134	T	?	138
RT	2730	150	RT	4133	90	RTL	975	133	T	600	49
RT	2765	150	RT	4153	119	RTL	985	89	T	701	128
RT	2770	31	RT	4179	147	RTL	1006	106	T	788	72
RT	2804	15	RT	4189	21	RTL	1030	50	T	790	119
RT	2818	110	RT	4233	124	RTL	1057	115	Tbus	97C	155
RT	2863	98	RT	4336	122	RTL	1098	28	Tbus	397C	110
RT	2868	0	RT	4403	83	RTL	1124	104	Tbus	752	153
RT	2885	17	RT	4434	134	RTL	1157	45	Tbus	1061	26
RT	2940	97	RT	4526	49	RTL	1206	57	Tbus	1474	51
RT	2952	13	RT	4528	138	RTL	1224	86	TD	35	87
RT	3068	74	RT	4542	105	RTL	1243	114	TD	49	78
RT	3104	70	RT	4552	30	RTL	1252	109	TD	58	76
RT	3149	52	RT	4613	100	RTL	1288	54	TD	63	78
RT	3169	69	RT	4679	122	RTL	1302	108	TD	64	78
RT	3180	90	RT	4744	145	RTL	1303	25	TD	67	75
RT	3226	145	RT	4773	136	RTL	1348	143	TD	67	78
RT	3278	76	RT	4798	56	RTL	1382	51	TD	73	78
RT	3280	135	RTL	3	131	RTL	1432	62	TD	103	82
RT	3305	125	RTL	33	79	RTL	1482	70	TD	104	55
RT	3339	89	RTL	67	107	RTL	1498	154	TD	110	76
RT	3484	42	RTL	75	103	RTL	1515	143	TD	122	53
RT	3598	63	RTL	149	99	RTL	1606	141	S/V	1035CD	65
RT	3615	47	RTL	163	127	RTW	3	64	S/V	393W	146
RT	3630	149	RTL	337	30	RTW	26	126	S/V	432GF	66
RT	3635	63	RTL	349	35	RTW	54	139	S/V	970J	132